THE CREATIVE ACTIVIST

MAKE THE WORLD BETTER, ONE PERSON, ONE ACTION AT A TIME

BY RAE LUSKIN

FOREWORD BY MARY MORRISSEY

ISBN 13: 9781940014661

Library of Congress Catalog Number: 2015940598

Printed in the United States of America

First Printing: 2015

19 18 17 16 15   5 4 3 2 1

Cover and interior design by Emily Shaffer Rodvold at Lift Creative.

Wise Ink Creative Publishing
837 Glenwood Avenue
Minneapolis, MN 55405
wiseinkpub.com

To order, visit itascabooks.com or call 1-800-901-3480. Reseller discounts available.

ACKNOWLEDGMENTS

The term Creative Activist was first coined by Kathy Eldon after her son Dan Eldon, an artist, adventurer, and activist, was killed in Somalia in 1993. To honor his legacy, Kathy founded Creative Visions Foundation to help others like Dan use media and the arts to create meaningful change around the world. I want to thank Kathy for her friendship and inspiration. To find out more, go to **creativevisons.org**.

I want to also thank the 120 exceptional leaders I interviewed. Your insight and candor helped frame The Creative Activist, even if your story was not highlighted in this book. Your vision and actions are making the world a better place. Thank you.

Many teachers helped me get to this place. I want to thank Vincent Toran, Felicia Searcy, and Mary Morrissey for their expert coaching.

Creating this book was quite an endeavor and I am deeply indebted to my wonderful team of editors, designers, and marketers: Amy Quale, Anitra Budd, Connie Anderson, Emily Shaffer Rodvold, and Jeane Heckert. Thank you for getting the message out to the world.

This book is dedicated to my granddaughters, and the Creative Activist in all of us.

TABLE OF CONTENTS

FOREWORD

Gandhi said, "You must become the change you wish to see in the world." This well-known quote can be found on many T-shirts and inspirational memos, but how can it really be applied in today's world?

We are in a unique time for activism, as there has never been a time in history when we have had so many challenges and opportunities for new "awake" and creative leaders to emerge. We have more avenues and technologies through which to share ideas than we ever have, giving ways to localize ideas and messages that can spread positive activism in ways never before seen. Yet, because of the mass influx of to-do's and information, many of us also feel like we're sleepwalking through life, hoping that someone else will step up to make the changes we want to see in the world. But what if being an activist simply meant being your truest self by using your own gifts? How would you live if your to-do lists became the "to-be" lists that reflected the mission and purpose of your soul?

This book you hold in your hands is more than a guide to activism . . . it is a pathway to fulfillment. So, reader, turn the page. Your soul's purpose just might be waiting.

Mary Morrissey

INTRODUCTION

Creativity and service saved my life.

As a fat, shy girl, I was the child whom no one wanted on the kickball team. I was the child who shuffled along with her head down and spoke in a whisper—but I lived this rich life in my imagination. In my mind I was a princess with long, flowing straight hair, and I wore a brightly colored tiara. My bedroom was magical, with stars, a magnificent dollhouse, and a wonderful tea set to entertain my friends. My very own fairy godmother gave me this magic lamp, and I got three wishes. One, I was thin. Two, I was an only child. Three, I was a famous artist.

My love of art started at age seven when I conducted Miss Rae's art school for my sister and her friends. Getting a new box of crayons—the smell of the wax, the feel of the wrappers, the names sky blue, violet red, and sea green—made me smile. In first grade, I won a contest, and my painting hung at Marshall Field's department store in Chicago. My picture was in the newspaper.

My artist grandfather was so proud of me that he invited me to his art studio. It was a lot of fun in the beginning, but soon it turned dark. He sexually abused me—and it went on for years. When I finally understood what was happening, I was too ashamed and embarrassed to come forward. Who would believe me that the pillar of the community was a pedophile? So I kept quiet.

However, I acted out in subtle ways. Mom used to brush my hair every night, and one day I said, "Don't ever touch me again." She never asked why. Then I painted people with no faces. No one asked why. I wrote a paper in high school about vene-real disease. No one asked why.

At college, a teacher told me I was a terrible painter, and I had no business being an art major. I lacked the self-esteem and confidence to fight him, and thus I became an art history major. I had no idea I had been suffering flashbacks while I was in the studio. I knew I was in serious trouble when I started dancing on tabletops at bars and writing poetry about death. When I was a senior, I dropped out of college and began a twelve-year journey into traditional talk therapy.

During therapy I began to paint again. I stayed up all night painting a portrait of a young girl in pain, in black and white and shades of gray. I called it *Keening Her Lost Innocence*. It was so emotionally raw, charged, and intense for me that for a very long time after-wards, I could not paint. To see my work, go to **raeluskin.net**.

Although I healed enough to get married and have a wonderful husband, two great chil-dren, and a beautiful home, I was suffering. I should be happy, but I wasn't, because I felt like I was living a lie. After I got my children off to school, I'd crawl back into bed and stay in a fetal position until they came home. At night I stuffed down my feelings with pints of ice cream and bags of cookies. I felt out of control, a complete failure. All I could think about was walking in front of a train to end the pain.

But I decided to live—to take my healing into my own hands. I read a thousand self-help books and began to journal. Every day I wrote three things I was grateful for and three "did wells"—those things that you might take for granted but in the midst of depression seem really hard, like washing your hair, cleaning the kitchen, or taking a walk. As a work-shop junkie, I traveled the world to hear inspirational and motivational people like Joan Boryshenko, Caroline Myss, Doreen Virtue, John Bradshaw, Ram Dass, Jack Kornfield, and Esther and Jerry Hicks. I did ART, a technique I developed to: **A**ccess the pain with scribbles and doodles; **R**eframe the story you are telling yourself; and **T**ransform into the person you want to be. I was able to release the pain, the sorrow, the unthinkable onto canvas and paper.

I learned in a twelve-step group that helping others/service would ease the pain of isolation and depression. Instead of spending my life asking, "Why me?" I turned it around and asked, "How can I use this experience to help others?" My parents were community activists and philanthropists. They believed it was our responsibility to repair the world, *tikkun olam*, so at age twenty-three, I immersed myself in organizations that supported Jewish leadership, healthcare, and vocational training. Eventually I found my own passion: working with nonprofits that improved the lives of women and children.

Over the last forty years, I have:

- Created artwork for a gun safety campaign for Congresswoman Jan Schakowsky of Illinois.

- Participated in numerous campaigns to end child sexual abuse, rape, domestic violence, and elder abuse.

- Marched in Washington, D.C., for stronger gun laws.

- Lobbied in Washington, D.C., and the state capitol at Springfield, Illinois, for a woman's right to choose.

- Designed a curriculum for healthy relationships, and a survey about violence in public schools.

- Produced a one-day conference on domestic violence as a public health issue.

- Spoke at churches, synagogues, and on blog talk radio, sharing my story and artwork.

- Created a short YouTube video called "The Healed Heart." **http://www. youtube.com/watch?v=PXA8kx-GRkw**

After years of merely surviving, I was thriving. People would say to me, "You seem different, you seem happier," and I was. People asked, "What is your secret? Could you help me?" I began teaching *Art from My Heart* to children, women, and families.

In a supportive environment, they learned to use their imagination, fully express themselves, and feel more confident, creative, and capable.

WHY THE CREATIVE ACTIVIST?

After I published *Art from My Heart,* I stopped teaching children and waited for a sign to show me what I should do next. I heard a whisper: interview a hundred leaders. Since that whisper, I have interviewed over 120 social entrepreneurs, community leaders, and creative change agents. For a while, I had my own radio show, *Stuck to Unstoppable.*

I heard stories of people ranging from age twenty-three to seventy-six who had a dream and made it happen. They are ordinary people doing extraordinary things. Many experienced challenges: from addiction to death, divorce, abuse, illness, and failed careers, they made their experiences count for something. They turned their pain into purpose. Others listened to their own whisper and used their gifts in service. Through *The Creative Activist*, I came full circle, bringing together the pieces of my heart and my soul's calling.

WHAT IS A CREATIVE ACTIVIST?

They are ordinary people who use their imagination, creative thinking, and unique expression to make a positive difference in people's lives, communities, and the world. They teach, bridge gaps, foster understanding, and take action to make the world a better place.

Essential characteristics of the creative activist:

- **Aware:** know who they are, their gifts, talents, and passions

- **Congruent:** live in alignment with their core values

- **Imaginative:** well developed sense of wonder, play, and curiosity

- **Optimistic:** hopeful and positive

- **Courageous:** persistent and tenacious, and act in the face of fear

- **Authentic:** share their personal stories of failure and triumph

- **Collaborative:** build capacity and skills in other people

- **Expressive:** artists, messengers, and storytellers

- **Visionaries:** dream big to make the world a better place

- **Committed:** to serving and awakening the highest potential in people, communities, and the world

WHY IS IT CRUCIAL TO THE WORLD?

Henry David Thoreau said, "The mass of men lead lives of quiet desperation." It is not quiet—it is glaring in every newscast. The "bad" news is a call to action. We can't continue in the same way, or we will continue to get the same results. People are starving for new voices, strategies, and ideas to improve their lives.

It is our opportunity to do something different by being the best and highest version of ourselves, happy, fulfilled, peaceful, and free; then we can become role models, mentors, and leaders of change. We can develop new visions and initiatives, which inspire and can sustain heroic endeavors to make our communities stronger, safer, and more dynamic. When we come from a sense of global responsibility, we are a human family, more similar than dissimilar, and we can rise up together to create more peace, harmony, and wellbeing in the world.

Whether you like to paint, journal, or save old photographs, or you can't draw a straight line with a ruler, there is a *creative* within you waiting to be rediscovered and set free. Creative expression has the power to heal wounds and nurture the soul. When we enter a flow state of complete absorption in a creative process, we open our awareness to new perceptions and perspectives. There is physical evidence to support increased blood flow, improved immune system, and a greater overall sense of wellbeing. When you take time to create, you shift your attention into something generative and life affirming.

Creative people are masters of innovation and resourcefulness. They ask new questions, generate new ideas, and treat the impossible as possible. They have the capacity to improvise and to create bricolage: creative problem solving using a variety of materials that happen to be available. The Apollo 13 mission, which launched April 11, 1970, is a dramatic example of bricolage. When the spacecraft was on its way to the moon, an oxygen tank exploded, scrubbing the lunar landing and putting the crew in jeopardy. Mission Control in Houston helped the on-board crew use their lunar module as a "lifeboat." Using spare parts, socks, and spacecraft canisters, they improvised a method to reduce the carbon dioxide concentration in the spacecraft. The mission ended safely on April 17, 1970.

Creativity is a learned skill set. According to brain plasticity studies, our brains are wired to be inspired. Creative and innovative practices such as brainstorming, meditation, journaling, artist dates, and brain dumps can build new brain synapses. Creativity cannot only be taught, but it can be developed. We can train ourselves to tap into our passion and imagination and create original initiatives for social change.

George Bernard Shaw said, "You see things; and you say, 'Why?' But I dream things that never were, and I say, 'Why not?'"

I say why not be the voice that starts courageous conversations. What do you dream of doing?

- Shine the light on women and children in need of social justice.

- Prevent child sexual abuse.

- Provide food and water during natural disasters.

- Educate people about the special-needs community.

- Offer peer support during illness.

- Create a sustainable planet.

- Help animals in need.

- Offer hope to women in prison.

When you finish reading the thirty-six remarkable stories in this book, you will be able to answer the following questions:

- What matters to you?

- What do you want to create?

- Whose lives do you want to touch?

- What do you stand for?

- What keeps you stuck?

- Are you living for yourself or for others?

- How can you impact future generations?

- What story can you tell that will be of service?

- What can you do, with what you have, to make a difference today?

HOW TO USE THIS BOOK

Consider this book a box of Cracker Jacks, and the prize inside is your fabulous life. The content is easy to follow. Each chapter contains six inspiring stories of creative activists. Following each story are three thought-provoking journal questions to guide you along a path of self-discovery, as well as a call to action step to ground you in the *ACT of Activism*. In many instances, I include my personal experiences as examples. The chapter concludes with a short poem to anchor the lesson.

You may choose to use this book in several ways:

- Read the entire book in a few days, noting which stories touched you, and come back to answer the questions.

- Read one story a day. Get up, walk around, contemplate the answers, and take action.

- Use the book as a creative catalyst for the day. Randomly pick one story, quote, or question. Notice how it applies to your life in that moment. The goal is to make the material your own.

- Get a buddy or gather several friends and go through the book together. Learning to connect and collaborate is a key component of being a creative activist.

There is no right or wrong way to use the book nor time limits. Each time you answer the questions and take action, you are strengthening your creative activist muscles. Some questions will be easy, while others might feel too hard, and you want to skip them. Sometimes the hardest questions are the ones that offer the most growth and insight. Be sure to celebrate your accomplishments.

TOOLS AND RESOURCES

Buy a notebook or journal in your favorite color. This will be a treasure map of your journey and ideas. Make it special and make it your own, maybe decorating the cover.

Find a quiet space that gives you privacy to do the work. Create an intention and set the space. Before I begin work I have a small ritual. I light a candle and place my hands over several special touchstones, while asking for divine guidance and creative flow. Many people enjoy music in the background. Experiment and play with what is right for you.

We are here to make a difference. A smile and a kind word can change lives. It doesn't matter if you are a stay-at-home mom, a student, a young professional, the CEO of a Fortune 500 company, or a retiree—you have a sphere of influence. You can be a role model, a mentor, or a volunteer—a creative activist. Your life story, your experiences, your skills and knowledge are invaluable. We need your voice to bring together the dreamers and the doers, the decision-makers needed to tackle challenges. We need out-of-the-box thinkers to encourage and collaborate with the changemakers and philanthropists. You have unlimited power to live the life you desire and to make the world a little bit brighter.

$C \times J$

THE WORLD NEEDS TO HEAR YOUR VOICE AND SEE YOUR VISION.

Inhale deeply and let your heart sing

Align with your passion and awaken your dreams

Take a step toward the impossible and leap into soul service

Stand in your brilliance, power, and purpose.

CHAPTER ONE

LEAD WITH LEGACY

"The legacy we live is part of the ongoing foundations of life. Those who came before leave us the world we live in. Those who will come after will have only what we leave them. We are stewards of this world, and we have a calling in our lives to leave it better than how we found it, even if it seems like such a small part."

–JIM ROHN

Legacy is the contributions you make to your family, friends, and community. It's how you invest your time, energy, gifts, and talents, while connecting with others on a deeper level about something that truly matters. It is using your unique voice and brilliance to create something of enduring value that will benefit people today and in the future.

Thinking about a legacy is absolutely worth your time, because we create a legacy whether it is intentional or not. Bonnie Ware, an Australian palliative care nurse who attends to patients in the last twelve weeks of their lives, recorded their dying epiphanies in a blog called *Inspirations and Chai*. She later shared the five most common regrets:

1. I wish I'd had the courage to live a life true to myself, not the life others expected of me.
2. I wish I hadn't worked so hard.
3. I wish I'd had the courage to express my feelings.
4. I wish I had stayed in touch with my friends.
5. I wish that I had let myself be happier.

I would add one more:

6. I wish I had done more to make the world a better place for future generations.

Last year I was at a function at Ravinia, an arts complex near my home that hosts the Chicago Symphony and artists such as Tony Bennett, Carrie Underwood, and Train. I was talking to a man in his mid-twenties, and I asked, "What legacy would you like to leave?" He looked at me funny and said, "I don't need to leave money to anyone." I explained that I was asking, "How would you like to be known and remembered? How would you make a difference in the world?" His face brightened and he told me, "I've spent time helping out in a refugee camp in Africa. If I could do anything, I would go back and help build a village for these kids."

It is important to know what gets you excited, what your passion is, and what matters most. Don't let other people's opinions and voices drown out your own voice. Imagine how different life would be, what choices you would make, if life were focused on following your heart. The choices we make are the stepping-stones of our life, and one by one will become the path of our legacy. This is why you need to choose wisely, and know how you want to be remembered.

ASK YOURSELF: WHAT LEGACY DO YOU WANT TO LEAVE?

- Living a life where my core values and actions are aligned.

- Being authentic and fully engaged in my life.

- Listening with compassion.

- Inspiring others to embrace their greatness.

- Mentoring someone how to use their gifts and talents.

- Asking courageous questions that lead to innovation.

- Encouraging people to creatively express themselves.

- Spreading love and kindness to people.

- Embodying forgiveness.

- Building a business based on my values.

- Being an advocate for a cause that is important to me.

- Paying it forward.

- Starting a movement.

For each of you it will look different. Whatever is calling your heart, take consistent action toward that legacy.

- Writer and director Mary Bonnett shines the light on women and children in need of social justice and community support.

- Producer Simon Weinberg has, for the last twenty years, promoted film as a tool for child-abuse prevention.

- Photographer Stacey Canfield helps people face serious illness and loss with compassion and courage.

- Real estate developer Richard Lackey provides food and water during natural disasters as a for-profit business.

- Community activist Connie Lee travels around the country filming survivors of child sexual abuse.

- Tim Wambach's passion is educating people about the special-needs community.

You are never too old or too young to begin to make the changes necessary to live from a place of integrity and intention. Don't live with regret. Be a creative activist.

"The choices we make about the lives we live determine the kinds of legacies we leave."

—TAVIS SMILEY—

MARY BONNETT

It's about how we treat our girls, and how we raise our voice.

Mary Bonnett created and cofounded Her Story Theater. Mary holds a BFA in theater arts, a BFA in English literature, and an MA in creative writing from Bath Spa University, England. She has won numerous awards for excellence and outstanding contributions in professional theater, writing, directing, and theater education.

WHY DID YOU START HER STORY THEATER?

When I stepped into this third phase of my life, not the final phase, I thought, "What can I do and what can I bring to the table?" I can direct, write, and organize theater. The next question was, "What is my passion?" Social justice for women and children. I created Her Story Theater, and decided to put it in Chicago's backyard. The mission is to shine bright lights on women and children in need of social justice and community support. The goal is three-pronged: 1) Raising awareness, 2) Getting an audience charged up to be proactive, and 3) To raise funds for a Chicago partner that's doing great work on that specific cause.

The first piece we did was on homeless women, and we partnered with Deborah's Place, a residential care facility for homeless women. We interviewed thirty women. I researched the topic to see what the issues are and who is homeless. I selected characters to represent the women out there: mentally ill, runaways, victims of domestic violence, migrant workers, the economically challenged, and the ex-cons. We set the play in a beauty spa and salon, and we used experienced salon staff working in real time. The ex-con was getting her hair done, the mentally ill person was getting a facial, the economically challenged woman was getting her makeup done, and so on. A musical cue moved people from cubicle to cubicle so they could hear the before-and-after stories. Photographs of homeless from the streets were part of the experience, which we sold to raise money for Deborah's Place.

The next play, *Shadow Town*, was a powerful, attitude-changing production on the nightmarish issue of sex trafficking impacting our young women and children in Chicagoland. It was based on two years of interviews with people involved with sex trafficking in Chicago: an undercover detective, social workers, vice squad, therapists, johns, pimps, and the girls trafficked. Uniquely woven with dance and music, this piece follows the lives of four young girls and their journey into the life of modern-day slavery: Marisol from Humboldt Park, Tatiana from the Westside, Samantha from Naperville, and Ling Ling from China.

> *Did you know in metropolitan Chicago, 16,000 to 25,000 women and girls are involved in the commercial sex trade annually, and the average age is 14?*

The next production, *Shadow Town II: The Johns*, looked at how pornography, prostitution, and sex trafficking affects the family. From the "innocent" bachelor party with thirteen men having sex with an underage girl, to a father playing out his sex fantasies, or the son who is a porn addict and unable to have intimate relationships, thinking he is in love with the prostitute.

Human trafficking is big business. Globally, it's a $32 billion economy that survives by feeding the desires of men who buy sex. In the Chicago area, the johns are young and old, single and married, and usually wealthy men from the North Shore. Denial is the one thing they have in common, as they perceive the girls want to have sex with them, that they enjoy it.

WHAT IS YOUR DEFINITION OF CREATIVITY, AND WHY IS IT SO IMPORTANT FOR CREATING CHANGE?

The arts address all our senses and our intelligences. They make us feel alive, and they reach deep inside us and fill us up. Live theater with a deep emotional connection to the human condition gets to the truth of who we are. In this case, it's a truth about what is going on in your own backyard. It allows us to step into the world of that person, see how the character deals with it and understands it emotionally and psychologically. When you take the journey with them, you come out much wiser.

WHAT IS THE LEGACY YOU WOULD LIKE TO LEAVE THE WORLD?

I would like to get my plays published and make them accessible nationwide. This would enable smaller cities and towns to have access to the material and use it to raise awareness and funds. I would also like to create documentaries to go along with the scripts.

MARYBONNETT.COM

Journal:

- What are your skills and talents?
- What do you do better than anyone else?
- What could you do to improve the lives of women and children?

Call to Action:

Learn the warning signs indicating a child is being trafficked:

- Unexplained gifts, jewelry, or cell phones
- Controlling boyfriends or relationships
- Vague stories about her or his whereabouts
- Marked changes in behavior and speech
- Hidden communication/emails/texts
- Unexplained school absences
- Runs away from home

The National Human Trafficking Resource Center (NHTRC) is a toll-free hotline available to answer calls from anywhere in the country, twenty-four hours a day, seven days a week, every day of the year in more than two hundred languages. NHTRC is operated by Polaris, a nonprofit, nongovernmental organization that works exclusively on the issue of human trafficking. Call 1-888-373-7888.

SIMON WEINBERG

*I can change the world
by making movies.*

SIMON WEINBERG IS CO-OWNER OF BIG VOICE PICTURES, AND OUTREACH DIRECTOR FOR BIG VOICE PICTURES'S FILMS. HE WAS ALSO COPRODUCER FOR *BOYS AND MEN HEALING*. SIMON HAS BROUGHT BIG VOICE PICTURES'S FILMS WORLDWIDE AS A TOOL FOR TRAINING AND ADVOCACY ON THE ISSUE OF CHILD-ABUSE PREVENTION. HE INITIATES AND ORGANIZES HUNDREDS OF SCREENINGS WITH COMMUNITY PANEL DISCUSSIONS AT UNIVERSITIES AND LEADING CONFERENCES INTERNATIONALLY, INCLUDING RECENT SCREENINGS AT PENN STATE DURING THE SANDUSKY TRIAL.

WHY DID YOU START BIG VOICE PICTURES?

My father told me, "Whatever you get, whatever you do in life, you have to give back." The key to life is giving more than getting every single day of your life. My passion in college was getting pollution out of California. As a park ranger, I raised millions of dollars to protect California's rivers. About twenty-two years ago, I met Kathy Barbini at a fundraiser, immediately felt something between us, and eventually she became my wife. She said she had left New York and her work with 20/20 and MTV behind because she was making a film. She needed to do good work in the world, which was exactly what I believed. She said it was called *The Healing Years*, about women's issues and sexual abuse prevention, and she needed to raise $5,000–$10,000 to get started. I had dated many women, and probably over 50–60 percent of them were abused as children—and many had told me their story. It was something I wanted to be a part of.

I had grown up in an affluent neighborhood in San Francisco. Francis Ford Coppola was my den leader. I decided to knock on the doors of the very wealthy people whom I grew up with, names we all know. They had no idea about this subject but were willing to come support me at a big fundraiser one night in San Francisco. That night, we raised the money to kick-start the film, which we finished in 2000. Maya Angelou endorsed it. We continued to create other movies about healing and helping people.

WHO ARE YOUR ROLE MODELS?

First, my wife, Kathy. When we made the film *Boys and Men Healing*, she interviewed David Lisak, a very famous forensic psychologist who has worked with rape crisis centers for the last twenty, thirty years. However, he had never shared his own story of childhood abuse. Cathy has a compassionate way of allowing people to turn that corner—and decide it's time to tell their story.

I also love Mother Teresa because she wasn't afraid of being with people who were different. People are rarely comfortable talking about or acknowledging people who suffer from mental illness, homelessness, or sexual child abuse. They step back and shy away from what is different. It is important for us as a human race to start shifting from treating them as "other" and different than us. If a homeless person walks across the street, look him in the eye. He is your neighbor, and we are all connected.

WHAT IS THE LEGACY YOU WANT TO LEAVE?

I look at our son, and he's definitely changing lives with his love of life and the smile in his heart. When I'm gone, he's going to keep doing that, and he'll do that with his children, like my father did with me, and his father before him. I have met many thousands of people face-to-face, and have given every one of them LOVE, which they will feel forever. Before we transform the world, we need to transform ourselves with love.

BIGVOICEPICTURES.COM

Journal:

- What messages did you receive from your parents about giving back?
- What makes you feel great about yourself?
- How are you going to transform your life with love?

Call to Action:

The next time you see a homeless person, walk up to her, look them in the eye, and say hello. Two years ago I saw a homeless man rooting through the garbage in the park. I bought a grocery gift card and handed it to him. That winter I saw him again, this time in the library, and bought him another card. Let me tell you, I was very uncomfortable, but I sat down across from him, and we had a conversation. He said, "I hope you're not mad that I used part of the money to buy treats for the dogs in the park." A man with nothing *was paying it forward.*

STACEY CANFIELD

*I thought I was drafted . . .
it was a wonderful experience that I
could never say no to.*

STACEY CANFIELD IS AN ACCLAIMED PHOTOGRAPHER, BRAND-MARKETING
CONSULTANT, AND BOOK AUTHOR. WITH OVER TWENTY-FIVE YEARS OF PHO-
TOGRAPHY EXPERIENCE, SHE HAS EARNED BOTH LOCAL AND INTERNATIONAL
ACCLAIM FOR HER ARTISTRY IN THE FINE-PORTRAITURE INDUSTRY. SHE HAS
BEEN A LEADER IN THE AMBASSADOR PROGRAM, AND IN 2010, SHE CREATED
SOUL SITTERS TO PROVIDE A COMFORTING PLACE OF COMMUNITY AS WELL AS
EXPERT INSIGHT FOR THOSE IN NEED OF GUIDANCE DURING A TIME OF LIFE
OFTEN NEGLECTED—THAT IS, BEFORE THE DEATH OF A LOVED ONE. TOGETH-
ER WITH CANDACE GEORGE CONRADI, SHE COAUTHORED *THE SOUL SITTER
HANDBOOK: WHAT TO DO WHEN A LOVED ONE IS DYING.*

WHY SOUL SITTERS?

Even at age nineteen, I was comfortable being with dying people in my family. While
most of my family avoided it, I ran toward death. There is a sacredness at being close

to death. I became the escort, held his hand, and helped him cross to this most holy place. I can only equate it to what it must be like give birth to a child, and that holy moment where this child appears.

I often talk to my Higher Power and ask, "What do you have for me?" About six years ago I heard, "You are here to help people die."

Basically it's not about you, it's about you leading other people to lead. It goes to the power of surrender. Are you willing to take the call? I think the space between passion and purpose is quite short.

WHAT IS THE PURPOSE OF YOUR LEADERSHIP?

I am here to raise awareness and help redefine how our culture approaches the subject of death and loss. I make sure people have tools to help them navigate the grieving and the healing process in time to say a "good" goodbye without regrets.

Some common concerns people share are:

- I am afraid of saying or doing the wrong thing, and need some guidance so my loved one feels supported, heard, honored, and loved.

- How can I feel comfortable with my fears and still be completely present when I see my loved one, especially for the first time?

- I am facing a serious illness or diagnosis, and I want my friends and family to be at ease in our relationship. How can I help them communicate and do this so our connection remains authentic and comfortable?

- I feel helpless as either the person facing loss or as the one supporting a loved one facing a serious challenge. I know I cannot change what is happening, but is there a way for me to feel relevant and of service?

- I feel alone. Are there any simple things I can do to reconnect to the people I love and care about?

WHAT IS THE LEGACY THAT YOU WANT TO LEAVE?

I want to help people have a more meaningful life. The closer you are to death, the more you get afraid. I want to fill the lonely and overwhelming gaps. I want to give people the courage to think more clearly, make wise choices, and connect with those they love.

SOULSITTERS.COM

Journal:

- What activity are you naturally good at?
- What passion could be your purpose in life?
- If you knew you only had six months to live, how would you spend your time, and with whom?

Call to Action:

Write your eulogy. Imagine it is your funeral.

- What do you want people to say about you?
- What are your achievements and what difference have you made?
- Whose lives have you touched?

An example would read:

> *Rae was a tireless activist improving the lives of women and children around the world. Her #1 bestselling book, The Creative Activist, began a movement in the workplace, colleges, and high schools. Her best practices and curriculum are still being taught around the country. She was a role model to her three beautiful granddaughters who have followed in her footsteps as social entrepreneurs and creative activists, and her beloved children continue her legacy of philanthropy*

with the family foundation. She will be missed by her friends and soul sisters, but her artwork and her award-winning documentary will live on.

When you have completed your eulogy, ask yourself, "Do my current actions take me closer or further from my vision? What do I need to change in my life to live my legacy now?" Challenge yourself to change one small thing each day. For example, I tend to pass over my accomplishments and compliments. They make me uncomfortable, and I don't take them in. Every night before I go to bed, I write three gratitudes: Jeane told me how she got lost in the stories, and they were so inspiring; spending the evening with Alexis, and she told me what a great job I did; walking Mia in the sunshine. Next, I write three wins for the day: made a donation to my favorite charity, walked ten thousand steps, and started a Creative Activist brainstorm and mastermind Meetup group.

RICHARD LACKEY

A great leader is someone who has a clear vision, is goal-setting and goal-achieving, but she or he also has a moral directive.

RICHARD LACKEY IS THE MANAGING DIRECTOR OF GREATWATER INVESTMENT MANAGEMENT, LLC, AND THE GREATWATER FUND, LP, WHICH BUILDS AND RENOVATES BOUTIQUE HOTELS IN EMERGING MARKETS WITH A FOCUS ON ADVENTURE RESORTS, UNIQUE EXPERIENCES SUCH AS LUXURY TREE HOUSES, AND PROFITABLE, SUSTAINABLE, ECO-FRIENDLY BUILDING AND DEVELOPMENT STRATEGIES. RICHARD IS THE FOUNDER OF THE GLOBAL FOOD EXCHANGE, A FOR-PROFIT COMPANY DEDICATED TO RESOLVING GLOBAL ISSUES REGARDING EFFICIENT SUPPLY OF FOOD AND WATER FOLLOWING NATURAL DISASTERS US-ING A CAPITAL MARKETS STRUCTURE.

WHAT IS THE GLOBAL FOOD EXCHANGE?

Did you know that the world has been hit by more than four hundred natural disas-ters *per year* over the past decade, resulting in a loss of 1.8 million lives and leaving

28 million homeless? The problem as I see it is twofold: 1) Manufacturers cannot produce the massive quantities of food and other supplies needed fast enough, and 2) Governments, NGOs (organizations that are neither part of a government or a conventional for-profit business), and other aid organizations don't have the funds to create and maintain the network of stored food, water, and other supplies that are needed during a disaster.

We manufacture "relief vaults," which are forty-foot custom containers packed with emergency aid such as food, water, and shelter. Each food vault contains 58,500 highly nutritious dehydrated meals with an incredible shelf life of over twenty years. The water vault contains cutting-edge technology capable of producing an impressive one hundred thousand gallons per day from dirty water, or even seawater.

The vaults are purchased through the Exchange by a network of distributors, including benevolently minded investment pension funds, foundations, and endowments, and held in strategic "hotspots" around the world, ready for rapid deployment by rail, truck, ship, or helicopter. When disaster strikes, these vaults are immediately made available for governments and NGOs who provide direct relief to victims.

WHAT INSPIRED YOU?

I worked full time as a paramedic. I used to see children who were repeatedly abused, and I would report it to the Department of Family and Children Services—and nothing would be done. Those same children came to the ER severely wounded, or dead. It was very frustrating. That's a good example of where the systems don't always work the way they're supposed to, but we certainly have opportunities to make them much, much better.

We have arguably at least 1.7 million slaves in the world today. Ninety percent of those are under fifteen years of age. We have little boys in India who are pulled off the streets and put to work in brick factories where they labor twelve to fourteen hours a day. They are fed just enough to keep them alive, and when they die, they throw them in the ditch out back. Then they get another child because there are millions of little boys running around the streets.

I feel this moral imperative to do something, to create systems when I see a problem. I support an organization called International Justice Mission, which is a group of attorneys and advocates that go into countries like Indonesia, China, Malaysia, and Latin America to rescue sex slaves, and we help build strong cases against traffickers, pimps, and other perpetrators and support their prosecution.

WHAT IS THE LEGACY YOU WOULD LIKE TO LEAVE?

I want to create businesses that solve social problems. We have the technology, the knowledge, and the resources to start solving some of the social ills that exist. Biblically, the hungry and the poor will always be with us. It doesn't mean you are going to eliminate hunger or poverty completely, but you can certainly create an environment as well as standards and systems to dramatically reduce it everywhere in the world. There's a huge amount to be done. It won't be done in my lifetime and it probably won't be done in my children's lifetime. A lot of opportunities exist for people to create successful businesses that impart socially benevolent goals.

GLOBALFOODSECURITYFUND.COM

Journal:

- What experiences have you had that inspired you to volunteer or make a donation to a cause?

- What could you do to eliminate hunger or poverty in your community?

- What eco-friendly ideas could you incorporate in your life?

Call to Action:

Write out your business idea/plan with socially benevolent goals. I began with, "Create a business with products and services that help women feel empowered. Donate 10 percent of the proceeds from the sale of my blessing cards to organizations that support sexual abuse awareness."

CONNIE LEE

Victims never "Forget it," and they never "Get over it."

CONNIE LEE IS THE FOUNDER AND DIRECTOR OF THE ALL-VOLUNTEER FAMILY AND FRIENDS FIGHTING AGAINST CHILD SEXUAL ASSAULT FOUNDATION (FAC-SA). THE FACSA FOUNDATION PROVIDES ATTORNEYS AND COUNSELORS FOR CHILDREN OF SEXUAL ASSAULT AND THEIR FAMILIES, AS WELL AS GUIDANCE AND RESOURCES, A SUPPORT GROUP, COMMUNITY EDUCATION, AND PREVEN-TION PROGRAMS. FASCA CREATED A VIRTUAL ART EXHIBIT, HIGHLIGHTING DIF-FERENT ARTISTS AND MUSICIANS, CALLED THE HOLOCAUST OF INNOCENCE WALL. IT IS PART OF THE SHATTERING THE SILENCE TOUR AND DOCUMENTARY PROJECT.

HOW DID YOU COME UP WITH THE IDEA FOR FASCA?

I grew up in an abusive home and married a very nice guy, but he ended up being an abusive person. After we divorced, I put my children through school and later put myself through college. However, I had this dream. I woke up at one o'clock in the morning with this vision for FACSA, doing an NBC show, and writing petitions to change pedophile laws. This is how the FACSA Foundation began.

WHAT ARE THE KEY ELEMENTS OF LEADERSHIP?

The number one key is never let your fears override your dreams, because you are going to face many obstacles. If you don't have the passion and the drive for this, you'll get burned out very fast, and perhaps you'll want to stop, especially if you aren't being paid. You know you are passionate when you continue, even if everybody else is burned out. You continue because you see the vision, know where you want to go, know the things you want to accomplish and the dreams and the lives you want to change. You must have love in your heart, as well as passion for people and community.

WHAT IS THE SHATTERING THE SILENCE TOUR?

We've been traveling the U.S. and Canada on a 115-city tour, filming a documentary on survivors' stories, conducting research on how child sexual assault is affecting our local communities, and hosting free public education prevention conferences across the nation on prevention of child sexual assault and human trafficking.

WHY ARE YOU DOCUMENTING SURVIVORS' STORIES?

We've been encouraging survivors to shatter the silence, and to regain the power they feel they have lost. It is so important for survivors to speak up, to tell, and not be a prisoner to fear. Ninety percent of victims know their perpetrators. It could be a family member, neighbor, or a community leader. Victims never "Forget it," and they never "Get over it." From the time of the traumatic incident the neural pathways of the brain have been altered, and until these processes have been worked through, usually with counseling, faith, or healing modalities such as creativity, the survivor will experience difficulty with trust and boundary issues, as well as displaying maladaptive behavioral issues.

WHAT KIND OF LEGACY WOULD YOU LIKE TO LEAVE?

The legacy I would like to leave would be having safer environments for children, for them to be able to grow in a happy, healthy home, and to fulfill their dreams. My ultimate dream is having two FACSA Foundation shelters in each state. These will be huge shelters with chapels, child screening, and self-defense classes. The apartments will have on-staff doctors, nurses, and security. The families can transition to a home, which they can rent or buy. That's my ultimate goal, and that will be my greatest legacy.

FACSAFOUNDATION.ORG

Journal:

- How have your wounds made you the person you are today?
- When have you had the courage to listen to a whisper/dream or intuition?
- What gets in the way of expressing your gifts and talents?

Call to Action:

Steven Covey said, "Writing or reviewing a mission statement changes you because it forces you to think through your priorities deeply, carefully, and to align your behavior with your beliefs."

Use these five steps to write your personal mission statement:

1. Prioritize your values.
2. Name your talents and skills.
3. List causes you strongly believe in.
4. Select a group you would love to work with.
5. Write your message.

For example: *My commitment is to surround myself with life-affirming, healthy, loving people who are committed to their inner work, and to make play, creative expression, wonder, and joy a priority. I am dedicated to living a life that serves a greater purpose. My mission is to use my teaching, art, and activism to educate, challenge, and enable communities to improve the quality of life for women, children, and families. I mentor, support, and empower women in their personal journey to stand fully, freely, and joyfully in their brilliance, power, and purpose.*

TIM WAMBACH

It will forever be my duty to help others see more than just a "chair" or a disability, but to see an individual who has a lot to offer.

TIM WAMBACH IS THE FOUNDER OF THE KEEP ON KEEPING ON FOUNDATION (KOKO). HE IS THE AUTHOR OF *HOW WE ROLL*. SINCE 2007, THE PROCEEDS FROM HIS BOOK HAVE HELPED PAY FOR EQUIPMENT AND THERAPY FOR EIGHTY PEOPLE WITH DISABILITIES BY PARTNERING WITH OTHER AREA SOCIAL SERVICE GROUPS. KOKO NOW HAS A TEAM OF OVER FIFTY YEAR-ROUND VOLUNTEERS, AND HOSTS SEVERAL FUNDRAISERS AND SPECIAL EVENTS EACH YEAR TO ASSIST AND RAISE AWARENESS FOR THOSE LIVING WITH SEVERE PHYSICAL DISABILITIES.

WHY DID YOU START YOUR FOUNDATION?

As an aide in an elementary school, I was hired to help Mike Berkson, a twelve-year-old with cerebral palsy. Because Mike has virtually no control of movement of his arms or legs, it was my job to help him do things he couldn't do for himself. I quickly discovered that Mike was different than most children his age. It wasn't because of his wheelchair or cerebral palsy, but it was his razor-sharp, quick-witted sense of humor.

One day I had this great idea. I would take Mike and his able-bodied twin brother, David, to Disney World. They would fly back—but I would run the 1,155 miles from Orlando to Chicago. I had never run for more than thirty minutes at a time, but I was determined to do something in a big way for my friend Mike, and bring attention to cerebral palsy.

After training with a professional long-distance runner for six weeks, I crossed the finish line at Glenbrook South in August 2005, greeted by a cheering crowd that included Mike, a high school junior. The run took thirty-one days, and I wore out six pairs of shoes. It was the hardest thing I have ever done. I threw everything I had into the run, blood, sweat, and tears, literally. I dug deep and realized I had been living my life at half-speed. Walking was exhilarating, but it was also agonizing. I knew I had to raise my game the rest of my life.

When I got back, I wrote about my experiences with Mike in *How We Roll*, and started the foundation. In 2007 Mike and I were asked to give speeches at different events, which were well received. They were making people laugh and think. The audience response was unanimous every time—people wanted more. Our message affected every audience, and *they loved us*.

In January 2010, we decided to take our educational speeches and turn them into a seventy-eight-minute theatrical show, *Handicap This!* We use our relationship as the thread, the catalyst. It's probably about 70 percent comedy and 30 percent is simply true grit, and we definitely push the envelope: we don't pull any punches, we're not politically correct, we tell it like it is. We're real.

Over eleven thousand people have seen our show, and it has been an incredible journey. Last week in Kentucky we did a show for fifth grade through seniors in high school. The teachers didn't want to go, thinking it was going to be a disaster, but after the show, the teachers said, "Wow, we're amazed at the show, at our kids' attentiveness throughout the program." A lot of people think it's a handicap show, and it's not at all. It's a life show, it's about dreams, it's about goals, it's about overcoming obstacles—and we all have that.

WHAT WOULD YOU TELL SOMEONE WHO SAID, "I DON'T KNOW WHAT I CAN DO TO MAKE A DIFFERENCE IN THE WORLD"?

You can do anything. It doesn't take a lot to find an opportunity because people need help all over this country. You can find something to do that would make a difference. You are not going to change the world overnight; it's going to be gradual, but the journey of a thousand miles begins with the first step. You can help when you're driving home from work, and you're on a toll way, you can pay for someone behind you, or you can volunteer for an organization that resonates with you. You can start your own organization. You could be a big brother to a young boy or a big sister, or you can go to a library and read books to children. There are so many different things anyone can do—it's not for lack of opportunity, it's for a lack of looking for the opportunities.

WHAT IS THE LEGACY YOU WOULD LIKE TO LEAVE?

I want Keep On Keeping On to be a household name. Mike and I want to be able to perform on Broadway and make a movie about our relationship. I want Keep On Keeping On to become a national organization, a household name long after I'm gone. Nonprofits need to be the leaders instead of the government, as far as giving out help to special-needs community.

KEEPONKEEPINGON.ORG

Journal:

- When was the last time you did something nice for someone, without him or her knowing it?

- How did it feel?

- Who have you met that has inspired you with their sense of humor or her courage during challenging times?

Call to Action:

I first heard the saying "Practice random acts of kindness and senseless acts of beauty" many years ago. I have been the recipient and the giver. I was in San Francisco attending an expressive arts conference, and I did not have enough cash to take the bus to the airport. I asked the clerk at the hotel if he could add money to my bill to cover it, but it was not their policy. Instead, he gave me $20 out of his pocket to cover the expenses. When I asked for his address so I could repay him, he said, "Pay it forward."

Here are twenty of my favorite acts of random kindness:

1. Smile at someone. You never know what he or she is going through, and it can make all the difference.

2. Allow someone to do something for you. It makes that person feel good.

3. Let someone merge in front of you in traffic.

4. Put your smartphone away, and give your child your undivided attention.

5. Speak to the homeless person on the street. Ask him what he needs, and get it for him.

6. Pay for the person behind you at the cash register.

7. Buy some balloons, and pass them out.

8. Give a cold bottle of water to the workmen in your neighborhood.

9. Donate via Twitter. Chirpify's donations platform allows people to donate to their charities of choice with one tweet.

10. One day, ride your bike or walk to work to lower your carbon footprint.

11. Read to a child.

12. When you walk your dog, pick up some other dog's poop.

13. Return a stray shopping cart.

14. Write a sticky note thank-you and leave it on your plate.

15. Start a "family kindness" journal.

16. Assist a senior in her garden.

17. Make a "build a bear" for a local charity.

18. Collect art supplies and books to take to the children's hospital.

19. Bake some cookies for your neighbor or coworker.

20. Make some appreciation cards, and pay them forward.

Make a list of twenty random acts of kindness. Commit to doing one every day.

Stand in Your Brilliance, Power, and Purpose

RAE LUSKIN

Inhale deeply and let your heart sing

Align with your passion and awaken your dreams

Take a step toward the impossible and leap into soul service

Stand in your brilliance, power, and purpose.

Illuminate your light and let dreams lead the way

Be authentic, empathetic, and a compassionate listener

Actively embrace a fail-forward attitude

Stand in your brilliance, power, and purpose.

Express your magnificence, not hiding any parts

Be clear about your calling and kind to your inner critic

Move through insecurity and begin deep transformation

Stand in your brilliance, power, and purpose.

Live a legacy of commitment and change

Be the torchbearer who ignites a special spark in others

Create something of enduring value and pay it forward

Stand in your brilliance, power, and purpose.

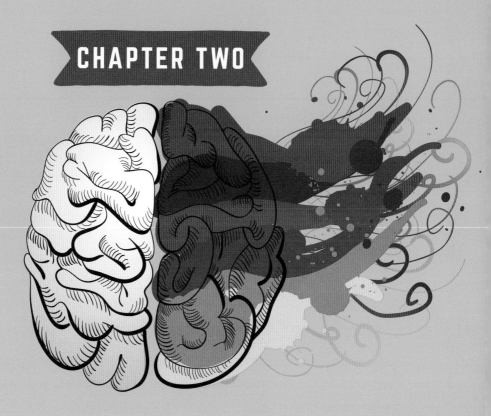

CHAPTER TWO

DISCOVER THE CREATIVE EDGE

"The creative is the place where no one else has ever been.
You have to leave the city of your comfort and go into the
wilderness of your intuition. What you'll discover will be
wonderful. What you'll discover is yourself."

—ALAN ALDA

We were born creative. We used to ask endless questions, much to our parents' dismay. We used to imagine, make up stories, and play pretend. We freely expressed ourselves in fun and exceptional ways. As children, we were told: the cow is not purple, stop fidgeting in your seat, stop daydreaming, and there is only one right answer. It is time once again to walk on the creative edge and play in the realm of your imagination, ask endless questions, and tap into your intuition to see opportunities, solve problems, and uniquely express yourself.

People who are able to step outside the boundaries of traditional thinking can generate new ideas, make superior decisions, and get bottom-line results. Steve Jobs once said that Apple flourished because the team members were poets, musicians, and artists who were also excellent computer scientists. The confluence of the arts and science can be found everywhere, from skyscrapers, to suspension bridges, to the gardens at Versailles.

Despite what you may think—"I don't have a creative bone in my body"—creativity is not the exclusive domain of artists, musicians, and professional designers. Artists are creative by nature, but you don't have to be an artist to be creative.

You are creative when you:

- Make a meal out of strange ingredients you find in the refrigerator.

- Plan a scavenger hunt in the house on snow days.

- Figure out how to attend your child's volleyball game and still meet your deadline at work.

- Rework the budget so you can fix the leaky roof.

- See a potential problem with your client's strategy, and diplomatically propose an alternate solution.

- Organize a clothes drive for a family in need.

Everyone has the ability to think creatively, problem solve, and generate more ideas. It requires practice, the same way you need to train your body for the marathon.

All too often, we let our brain go on auto\pilot through repetitive routines and rigid thinking and fail to nourish our curiosity. Don't rush through your day, but rather indulge in play, wonder, and joy. Notice what is happening right outside your window, and do so with the eyes of a six-year-old. Ask questions. Be surprised. By assuming a new perspective, you open yourself to discovery, learning, and your creative potential.

TAKE A WALK ON THE CREATIVE EDGE.

- Prioritize fun, stimulating physical space with entrepreneur Eva Niewiadomski.

- Take time for brain dumps and artists dates with Sarah Thurber.

- Learn how to vision with best-selling author and expressive arts therapist Lucia Capacchione.

- Receive tips and tools to generate fresh ideas with educator Cory Wright.

- Overcome blocks with creativity coach Gail McMeekin.

- Practice sacred art and healing rituals with art medicine woman Aviva Gold.

"The real voyage of discovery lies not in finding new landscapes but in having new eyes."

—MARCEL PROUST—

EVA NIEWIADOMSKI

The number one tenant of our philosophy here is that environment matters and that creative environment helps individuals tap into the deep reserves of their imaginations.

EVA NIEWIADOMSKI IS A SUCCESSFUL ENTREPRENEUR WHO CREATED A NEW CATEGORY IN THE HOSPITALITY INDUSTRY, CREATIVE CONFERENCE SPACE, WHEN SHE OPENED CATALYST RANCH. IT IS HOUSED IN A HISTORICAL LOFT IN DOWNTOWN CHICAGO AND WHIMSICALLY FURNISHED WITH VINTAGE FURNITURE, ETHNIC ARTWORK, COLORFULLY PAINTED WALLS, TOYS, BOOKS, AND MUCH MORE. IN 2008 CATALYST RANCH WAS NAMED TO *INC. MAGAZINE'S* TOP 100 FASTEST-GROWING PRIVATE COMPANIES IN ILLINOIS. PRIOR TO STARTING HER OWN BUSINESS, EVA SPENT ALMOST TWENTY YEARS IN CORPORATE, WORKING FOR THE QUAKER OATS COMPANY IN A VARIETY OF FINANCE AND MARKETING POSITIONS, AND AT ARTHUR ANDERSEN & CO.

WHY DID YOU START CATALYST RANCH?

When I started Catalyst Ranch in 2002, it was with the thought that there was a different way to enable creative thinking. At Quaker Oats I had created different spaces, a couple of innovation hallways and a creativity room as a sideline to my day job. I decorated my desk, I had a lot of artwork around, and people loved coming and having meetings at my desk. There was a different energy in how we approached things because there was a different physical environment.

Many people take for granted the importance of a creative, fun space. They don't understand how important it is to engage the brain in a different way to get better results. Too often in a plain conference room people zone out, and it doesn't matter whether you are training someone, or having a strategic planning or product ideation meeting.

If you come here for a meeting, you will experience it for yourself. You can see and feel the difference in your energy level and the output of your meeting here versus when you've done similar meetings elsewhere. We show people how a creative environment impacts them, and hopefully helps them come up with greater products, achieve better strategic direction, and come up with ideas they wouldn't have come up with otherwise. In addition, they learn that a creative space is an important component of your day-to-day life, and certain changes need to happen within your corporate environment.

WHY DO WE NEED TO GIVE PEOPLE PERMISSION TO HAVE FUN?

There's a corporate mantra, "If we are doing serious business, we have to be serious." On the other side is the idea that if you are having fun, you can't possibly be working as hard as you should be. I think this is counterproductive. When people are playing, having fun, thinking in a very different way, and being more creative, they have realized better approaches to whatever their assignment is.

We want to make sure Catalyst Ranch employees are having fun and enjoy working with each other. We have a lot of things to do that are mundane in terms of writing contracts, setting up meetings, talking with people, making sure their rooms are set up correctly, and dusting the room. I hire creative people who are actors, artists, photographers, musicians, filmmakers, and writers. I think it's important that employees have other interests and passions, and they bring that to their day-to-day life. That's what makes them interesting. It's what builds the dynamics between the staff, and it's where we get some of our best ideas.

CATALYSTRANCH.COM

Journal:

- What were your favorite childhood toys?
- What ways can you enhance your physical space to be more stimulating and fun?
- What rewards and incentives would encourage innovative thinking?

Call to Action:

Do you remember when you were a child, and you knew you could save the world? You were invincible when you tied a towel around your neck and you became Superman, Wonder Woman, or Batman. Your imagination was bristling with ideas. Take a few moments to see yourself as the superhero of your own life adventure.

- What superpowers do you have?
- What is your mission?
- What do people say about you?
- What costume do you wear? Do you wear a mask?
- Does it hide or reveal your true identity?
- Do you have a base of operation?
- Do you have a sidekick or do you work alone?
- Who are the bad guys in your world, and what do they look like? Do you have a creed or motto you live by?

Let your imagination run wild and have fun. After you have a clear picture of your adventure, write about it, and draw yourself as a superhero.

LUCIA CAPACCHIONE

The most important thing I learned at college was how to dream, and how to turn a vision into reality.

LUCIA CAPACCHIONE, PH.D., A.T.R., R.E.A.T., IS THE BEST-SELLING AUTHOR OF EIGHTEEN BOOKS AND AUDIO CDS. AFTER SUCCESSFUL CAREERS IN BOTH ART AND EDUCATION, SHE STUMBLED ONTO THE HEALING POWER OF ART AND JOURNALING USING HER NONDOMINANT HAND WHILE STRUGGLING WITH A MYSTERIOUS LIFE-THREATENING ILLNESS. SHE RECOVERED WITHOUT MEDICATION, WHICH LED TO THE CREATIVE JOURNAL METHOD THAT BLENDED WRITING WITH DRAWING, AND WAS A PIONEER IN INNER CHILD/INNER FAMILY HEALING THROUGH JOURNALING AND EXPRESSIVE ARTS. SHE CONDUCTS WORKSHOPS AND PROFESSIONAL TRAINING USING HER INNOVATIVE METHODS FOR SCHOOL SYSTEMS, VETERANS, CANCER SUPPORT GROUPS, AND MENTAL HEALTH AND RECOVERY CENTERS. DR. CAPACCHIONE HAS CONSULTED FOR CORPORATIONS, INCLUDING MATTEL, HALLMARK, AND WALT DISNEY IMAGINEERING.

HOW DID YOU GET STARTED IN THE ARTS AND LEADERSHIP?

I studied with Sister Mary Corita at Immaculate Heart College, who was best known for her pop art posters blending scripture, poetry, and advertising. There I learned to dream, and how to turn a vision into reality.

I wanted to work for world-famous designer, architect, and filmmaker Charles Eames when I finished college. As a student, we made field trips to his home and office. I kept imagining myself working in the office. My daydreaming paid off, and my junior year I worked there part time and was offered full-time work upon receiving my bachelor's degree. Many of the design principles I learned from Charles and his staff inspired my ten-step visioning process.

WHO ELSE INSPIRED YOU?

My second great mentor was inventor and philosopher R. Buckminster Fuller. We became friends when I began my second career as a Montessori-trained child development specialist, and one of the first Head Start directors in 1965 in Los Angeles after the Watts riots. Bucky taught me to look deep below the surface and find light in the darkest of times, as he had to do after the death of his first child.

Finally there was Walt Disney. I never met him, but I consulted with his Imagineering team for ten years. I love this story. One day Walt was at a kiddy carnival with his children, and he started playing the "what if" game. What if there was a place where children and adults could come together and have fun? What if there were rides and amusements everyone could enjoy? "What if" became "why not" and the birth of Disneyland. That is how I approach life: what if?

WHAT IS VISIONING®?

It is a practical way to make your dreams come true. It is a creative process that applies imagination to the real world. Through collage, drawing, and writing with the nondominant hand, you can find your true heart's desires and make them a reality.

Architects and designers create 3-D models and blueprints when they get an idea.

They don't sit around visualizing it in their minds. I examined the steps that designers use and broke them down into ten steps, starting with making a wish and ending with celebrations when the dream becomes reality. The key is to stop worrying how the dream will manifest. Your job is to get clear about what you want by illustrating it through a collage, to reinforce it daily by looking at the collage, to deal with the inner doubts with journal prompts, and allow it to happen in its own way. That last one is tough. When you do that, the path becomes so much more creative and surprising than you could have ever imagined.

Ask yourself, what is my true heart's desire at this time in my life? The ten steps are:

1. Make a wish or set an intention.

2. Search for images and words that depict your deepest desire.

3. Focus on the vision while sorting through your cutouts.

4. Compose the design: arrange your images on poster board or paper.

5. Explore and find order in creative chaos: address the voice of doubt and fear with journaling.

6. Create the collage and glue down your words and images.

7. Articulate the vision and write impressions, thoughts, and feelings through journal prompts.

8. Reinforce the dream: look at your vision every day.

9. Embrace the reality and surround yourself with support.

10. Celebrate the dream come true.

LUCIAC.COM

Journal:

- What are your earliest memories of being creative or imaginative?
- What messages did you receive from teachers and parents about creativity?
- Which messages do you believe and which ones can you discard?

Call to Action:

Begin working on your vision using the ten-step process. Experience has taught me that when you start something new, your inner critic is bound to show up in the form of self-sabotage, and you decide you need to clean your apartment before you can sit down to work. Or this voice in your head says, "I'm too young, too old, why bother because things never go my way." These fear thoughts will interfere with your ability to feel confident and empowered and to make a difference. For the next ten minutes, write everything your inner critic is saying to you about your vision, and write in the second person, doing so with your dominant hand. Ask your inner critic, "What do you want me to know?" and answer with your nondominant hand. Acknowledge and thank your inner critic. By acknowledging fear, you can push it to the edge of your consciousness and take positive action toward your dreams.

CORY WRIGHT

I strive to bridge the gap between industry and education.

CORY WRIGHT, M.S., IS AN EDUCATOR AND PARTNER WITH ZIDEAS CREATIVITY AND INNOVATION GROUP. SINCE THE NINETIES, HE HAS BEEN IMMERSED IN THE FIELD OF CREATIVITY AND LEARNING, TEACHING AND IMPACTING ORGANIZATIONS AND PUBLIC EDUCATION. CORY AUTHORED CASE STUDIES FOUND IN THE BOOK *CREATIVE LEADERSHIP: SKILLS THAT DRIVE CHANGE.* SINCE 2006, HE HAS PRESENTED REGULARLY AT EVENTS AND CONFERENCES, AND DESIGNED THE REAL WORLD TEEN CREATIVE LEADERSHIP CONFERENCE OFFERED BY THE NONPROFIT CREATIVE LEADERSHIP AMERICA.

WHAT IS CREATIVE LEADERSHIP AMERICA?

Creative Leadership America seeks to meet the challenge of developing the next generation of leaders in the greater Rochester, New York area. This program presents a one-of-a-kind conference offering a three-day immersive experience with real business clients and real challenges for young people from ages fifteen to nineteen. The participants learn a mindset, toolset, and skillset necessary to inspire creativity and drive positive change.

Two stories that drive home the value and the power of the experience: One student went to college and contacted me. "Well, Cory, my team broke the school record for community service. I took the process you taught us, and we came up with all these actions, and how we could generate community service hours. We implemented it all, and we broke the record."

Another student had to leave school because of drug-related problems, and when she returned, she was given an independent project based on *How to Win Friends and Influence People*. We went through the book and looked at each principle, and we changed the words to be more teen-friendly. We reorganized it, and came up with teen-related examples and stories. For instance, under "Six Ways to Make People Like You," it says to remember that a person's name to that person is the sweetest and most important sound. What happens when you forget their name? You feel embarrassed. We came up with a curriculum and a journal with more hands-on exercises and cartoons to illustrate the principles. We built an assessment so the teens could see how they were applying the material in real life. It was so successful we got a grant for teachers to use it in schools.

WHY DO YOU THINK IT IS IMPORTANT TO TEACH CREATIVITY IN SCHOOLS?

Right now it is all about right or wrong. I think we need to teach children observation and evaluation skills based on the question: what is good about this? I've been blown away by how many products have emerged because somebody saw the value in a novelty. The Popsicle was invented in 1905 by eleven-year-old Frank Epperson on a cold night in San Francisco. He left a stir stick in a mixture of powder-flavored soda water on the porch, and when he woke up he had a frozen treat. George de Mestral in the 1940s took a walk in the woods and noticed the tiny hooks on the cockleburs that stuck to his legs and his dog's fur. From that observation, Velcro® was invented.

I always evaluate what is good or useful before what is wrong and needs to be improved. I applied what might be good about this principle with my daughter Grace when she was six. She would get upset and frustrated pretty easily, and we decided to write a book together about this, which she named *Oh Shucks, I Got It*. Here's an example. She was drawing and she ripped the paper, so she crumpled it and threw it away. We grabbed the paper out of the trash and asked what might be good in here. She was working on a Christmas picture, and she decided she could use the crumpled paper to add texture to her mountains. Grace said, "I got it." She transformed the bad thing into something good.

HOW DO YOU TAP INTO YOUR CREATIVITY?

One technique is forced connections. It is based on the brain's ability to link two entirely different words or objects, and then use them to think through a problem. For instance, I am writing a book, and I want to find unique ways to market it. I go through all the traditional ways, but they just aren't working for me. I am at my computer looking at my mouse, a random object, and I ask myself a series of questions about the mouse. What do I notice about the mouse? What are the characteristics of the mouse? How is this like my problem? What are the similarities? You never know what it will trigger. You don't censor your thoughts and you write them down. What if I created a mouse mascot to represent my book, and I let him loose on the building? Looking at the rounded shape of the mouse, I wonder why folks are always squared up? Why don't we create a rounded book that is visually going to stand out from everyone else?

ZIDEAS.COM

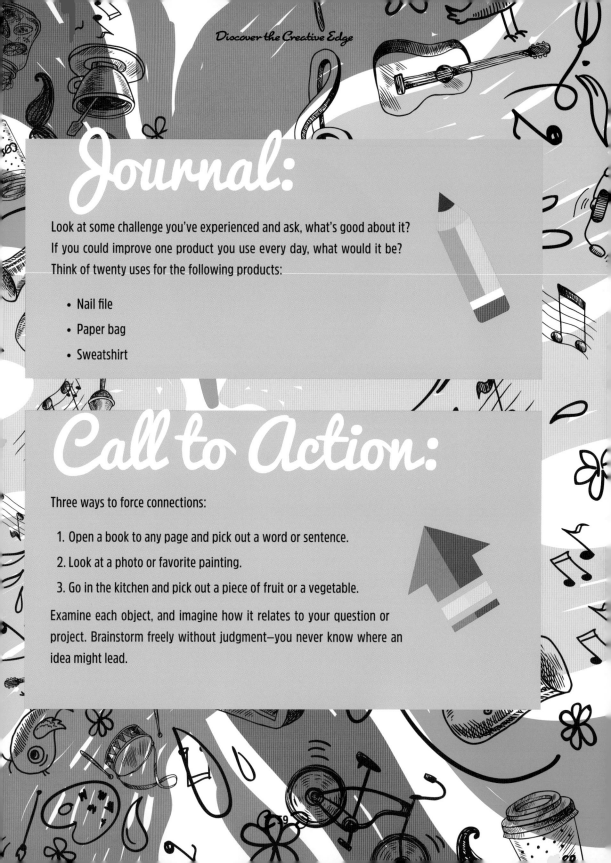

Journal:

Look at some challenge you've experienced and ask, what's good about it?
If you could improve one product you use every day, what would it be?
Think of twenty uses for the following products:

- Nail file
- Paper bag
- Sweatshirt

Call to Action:

Three ways to force connections:

1. Open a book to any page and pick out a word or sentence.
2. Look at a photo or favorite painting.
3. Go in the kitchen and pick out a piece of fruit or a vegetable.

Examine each object, and imagine how it relates to your question or
project. Brainstorm freely without judgment—you never know where an
idea might lead.

GAIL MCMEEKIN

We need to have environments where people aren't afraid to express their opinions or worried about getting laid off.

GAIL MCMEEKIN, LICSW, IS A NATIONAL EXECUTIVE, CAREER, AND CREATIVITY COACH, AS WELL AS A LICENSED PSYCHOTHERAPIST AND WRITER LOCATED IN BOSTON. WHEN SHE WAS THIRTY-FIVE, SHE WAS DIAGNOSED WITH CHRONIC FATIGUE SYNDROME, AND FOUND THAT ART, BEAUTY, AND CREATIVE EXPRESSION HELPED HER HEAL. AFTER YEARS OF REDECORATING, ADDING COLOR TO HER WARDROBE, AND PAINTING WATERCOLORS, SHE STARTED COACHING CLIENTS ON HOW TO LEVERAGE THEIR CREATIVE IDEAS INTO HEARTFELT, PROSPEROUS BUSINESSES AND FULFILLED LIVES. SHE IS THE AUTHOR OF *THE 12 SECRETS OF HIGHLY CREATIVE WOMEN: A PORTABLE MENTOR* AND THE COMPANION CALLED *THE 12 SECRETS OF CREATIVE WOMEN JOURNAL*. HER NEWEST BOOK IS *THE 12 SECRETS OF HIGHLY SUCCESSFUL WOMEN: A PORTABLE LIFE COACH FOR CREATIVE WOMEN*.

HOW DO YOU NURTURE CREATIVITY?

I was really lucky that I was able to take a creativity workshop with George Prince, cocreator of Synectics, an innovation consulting firm, and his wife, Kathleen Logan Prince. Through their Mind-Free program, I learned about the positive power of mistakes and our self-imposed limitations. It transformed my fear of being wrong. I learned that making mistakes is part of the creative process. It is important to give people permission to do that. To create an environment where you go out on a limb and try something, maybe it doesn't work, but you recognize it still leads you to the next thing. Whatever you learned from that project that didn't work leads you closer to the answer. We need to have environments where people aren't afraid to express their opinions or worried about getting laid off.

WHY IS QUIET CRITICAL TO CREATIVITY?

When you are trying to look at something with a new lens—trying to solve a problem, invent something new—you have to divorce yourself from all those inner and outer distractions. We need to have mixed spaces that allow people, depending upon their personality and the kind of work they are doing, to have quiet time, which is why some companies are doing quiet spaces. It's almost impossible to concentrate in these modular offices where you can hear your neighbor talking about her symptoms as she's making an appointment for the gynecologist. People are so bombarded with noise they can't get grounded and centered in their thinking. I often coach my clients to go out in their car for a while, or hang out in the conference room. On the commuter rail here in Boston, they have quiet cars where you are not allowed to talk to others, or on the phone.

HOW DO YOU TAP INTO YOUR CREATIVE GENIUS?

I find journaling to be grounding, and I use different kinds of journals for different things. I carry a journal for each book or product that I'm working on and write down anything that pops into my head. I use a lot of sticky notes. Whenever I get an idea, I write it on the note and put it in the basket in my office, which I review quarterly.

Sometimes I drive to a private beach, and nobody is there but the birds, and I will paint. I tend to paint on tiles because if you don't like what you did, you wash it off in the water. I find painting and collaging stimulate my creativity. I make what Julia Cameron calls artist dates wherein I explore something new, read something totally different, and have a whole new experience. My husband and I love to travel. With my iPhone 5, I can now take my own pictures of an incredible sunset in Maui and with a click, I can share and post them on the website. I've started doing SoulCollage®, which is a fun and creative collage process. You make your own deck of cards, and each collage card represents one aspect of your personality or soul.

WHAT DO YOU DO WHEN YOU GET STUCK?

When I get stuck on a problem, I sit down and paint a picture of whatever I think is going on in my head, which I do a lot when I write a book. When I am painting, I have to leave my inner critics outside the door. I've done a home study right-brain drawing program. I continually need to be learning. I have a section in my success book where I talk about filtering and focusing, and letting go of things that aren't working. I find decluttering also very stimulating. About six weeks ago I took every single thing out of my filing bookcases, cleaned it, donated all kinds of stuff to the library, gave things to friends, threw some out, and organized by topic. It was helpful to take everything out and to think carefully about what I put back.

CREATIVESUCCESS.COM

Journal:

- What do you say to yourself when you make a mistake?

- When have you failed, and realized it led you to answers down the road?

- How do you keep track of your ideas?

Call to Action:

Declutter. Make a list of all the things you want to organize or declutter. Devote fifteen minutes every day until it is done. I find it challenging to file, sort, and throw away. I need support or I just shuffle papers from one pile to another. Ask a friend to help you or hire a professional organizer. I have done both. Check out **napo.net**.

AVIVA GOLD

Everyone is an artist, be it sculptor, singer, dancer, actor, musician, or poet, and anyone can be transformed by creative engagement, anywhere at any time.

AVIVA GOLD, AN ART MEDICINE WOMAN AND TEACHER, HAS FACILITATED AND LED INSPIRED PAINTING FROM THE SOURCE WORKSHOPS AND TRAININGS IN THE U.S. AND INTERNATIONALLY FOR THIRTY YEARS. SHE IS A MOTHER OF THREE SONS, AND HAS A BACKGROUND IN PSYCHOANALYTIC, JUNGIAN, AND GESTALT PSYCHOTHERAPY. HER FIRST BOOK, *PAINTING FROM THE SOURCE: AWAKENING THE ARTIST'S SOUL IN EVERYONE*, WAS PUBLISHED BY HARPER COLLINS IN 1998. AVIVA'S SECOND BOOK WAS SELF-PUBLISHED IN 2011, *SOURCE ART IN THE WORLD: HOW YOUR AUTHENTIC CREATIVITY HEALS THE PLANET*. IN 2013, AVIVA GOLD, ELISE CROHN, AND MEGO JOHNSON ESTABLISHED CREATIVE PASSAGE: ARTS TO RE-ENCHANT PEOPLE AND PLANET, A 501(C)(3).

WHY PAINTING FROM THE SOURCE?

Before my fifth birthday, I was sent from my tenement in Queens, New York City, to summer camp in the Catskill Mountains for two months. My mother said camp would protect me from the polio epidemic that ravaged New York City.

In camp I was dying of loneliness, and I was rescued by my imagination. They gave me paint to make pictures, a black pony named Molly to feed and brush, and allowed me to sit alone in a magic brook where good fairies sang to me from the rushing water. I saw stars in the black night sky for the first time, heard folk songs, and watched the miracle of my pea seeds grow into vines offering juicy pea pods to eat. Drawing and painting pictures and being in nature saved my life, and the seeds of a gypsy life as an art medicine woman were planted.

In 1983 I took a five-day "painting naturally" retreat. I met myself with so much resistance. I had to let go of tons of judgment about not being a great artist. As I painstakingly worked through the first few days, I had a breakthrough. I painted my version of God, Goddess, and Creation. For the first time, I understood the word "transformation." Each painting offered me opportunities to confront issues that plagued me for years. My anxiety attacks and my arthritis disappeared when I completed certain paintings. Tapping into my creative source made me feel worthwhile and I started taking better care of myself, eating right, and exercising.

I believe all creative expression is a sacred, healing activity, a two-way portal to and from the Divine. After years of witnessing profound transformation occurring in people's lives when they opened to the intuitive creative process, it became clear that experiencing authentic creative expression and ritual was a spiritual experience that exposed us to a deeper connection with each other, and to *all* creation.

I love teaching people. I love to show them how to get out of their own way and lead. I use the creative process to push people beyond what they think are their limits, and bring forth an altruistic vision.

WHAT IS YOUR PASSION TO LEAD NOW?

I inspire and motivate people to live a sustainable lifestyle that is more in tune with the needs of our planet, while also encouraging people to spread this inspiration to others.

HOW DO YOU INSPIRE PEOPLE?

I use ritual and creative expression. We combine a community art event with the cleanup of a vacant lot or beach. Using discarded items, we make a community sculpture, a story, or a book; with the broken pottery and glass, we can make a mosaic. We bring drums, rattles, and tambourines, and people join us.

You can designate a day when everybody practices art: group murals, poetry workshops, mob flash dances, and music events, with audience participation honoring the Earth. Have local churches involved. Call on local native tribes to officiate with their traditional blessings. Get local media involved.

PAINTINGFROMTHESOURCE.COM

Journal:

- In what ways can you bring creative expression to something you care about?
- What are you doing to improve the planet?
- How are you using ritual in your life?

Call to Action:

In Native American tradition, as well as many other ancient cultures, shamans or spiritual leaders would guide people on an inner journey to meet what they would call their spirit guide or power animal. Dancing and drumming would lead them into an alternate state of being or consciousness. They would gain valuable information from their guides that were not normally accessible. They consider art a sacred practice. By using deep breathing and visualization you can manifest your own vision. Gather some art materials: oil pastels, crayons, markers, Bristol board paper. Find a quiet place, let your imagination flow freely, and don't worry if the images are different than what you might see in the real world. Allow the images to unfold.

Close your eyes, sit comfortably with your feet on the floor and your hands in your lap. Inhale through your nose, and exhale through your mouth. Notice how the air tickles the back of your nose. Watch the rise and fall of your chest as you breathe in and out several more times. You are now ready to go on a journey. Imagine you are walking in a deep forest, and the sun is creating beautiful shadows on the ground. The silence is stunning. Notice a deer drinking at the water's edge. See the ripples forming on the water; they are mesmerizing.

Sit down on a boulder and feel the wind on your face. Feel the connection to Mother Earth. Ask your Spirit Guide or power animal to come to you. The guide may come in any form. What does it look like, what does it sound like? Begin a conversation, asking, "What is your message for me? How can I serve you? What is my world work?" Keep going back and say, "Tell me more about that." When you feel complete, say goodbye. Promise to keep in touch, and suggest your guide drop in whenever there is something important for you to know. Rest for a moment in this special place. Know your guide is wise, and has only your best interest at heart. When you are ready, open your eyes and begin to draw whatever images came to you. Let go of judgment—this is only for you. Write about your drawing. What did you learn from the experience, what are your next steps, what do you need to change about yourself?

SARAH THURBER

I think creativity is like a muscle.

SARAH THURBER IS MANAGING PARTNER OF FOURSIGHT, LLC. SARAH HAS A RICH BACKGROUND IN LEADERSHIP, PROFESSIONAL EDITING, AND INFORMATION DESIGN. FOR THE LAST TEN YEARS, SARAH HAS WORKED IN PARTNERSHIP WITH ACADEMIC RESEARCHERS AND TOP INNOVATION CONSULTANTS TO DEVELOP THE FOURSIGHT "THINKING PROFILE" ALONG WITH A RANGE OF OTHER TRAINING TOOLS THAT SUPPORT COGNITIVE DIVERSITY AND CREATIVE PROBLEM SOLVING. TODAY, SHE IS THE PRODUCER OF THE "FOURSIGHT CREATIVE THINKING TIP," WHICH HAS BEEN LICENSED BY GROUPS, INCLUDING AARP. SHE HAS COAUTHORED TWO TEXTBOOKS USED BY THE INTERNATIONAL CENTER FOR STUDIES IN CREATIVITY, WHERE SHE RECEIVED A MASTER OF SCIENCE DEGREE IN CREATIVITY.

CAN WE DEVELOP CREATIVITY?

Creativity is like a muscle. Some people think of it as a gift: you either have it or you don't. Research shows that everyone has this creative gift, but the unwrapping of it is difficult for some people. There are four types of creative: clarifier, ideator, developer, and the implementer.

Most people look at the person who generates lots of ideas as creative, and rarely recognize how the "doer" or the analytic who doesn't necessarily like to sit around and think of new things contributes to the creative process. I help people realize their own potential and unwrap that gift of creativity so they can apply it in their own life, and get such joy and energy from it. Our assessment tool shows you not whether you are creative, but how you are creative.

HOW DO YOU GET UNSTUCK?

Part of what I have spent the last fifteen years or so doing is packaging information and tools about how to get unstuck. It's like exercise, where you have to put your gym shorts on and do it. When I get stuck, I'll sit with a blank piece of paper and draw the thing in the middle that's the most overwhelming, whether its work related or something with my family. I'll put the problem right in the center, and create a mind map of the things attached to it, including what we have done so far, and what is overwhelming me. Sometimes when I am emotionally overwrought, I will write what Julia Cameron called morning pages. It's a brain dump, three pages handwritten, which I can throw out at the end. I also believe you need to eat well and exercise.

HOW DO YOU GET INTO THAT SPACE OF INSPIRATION?

If you are looking directly at a star that's far, far away, it's hard to see it sometimes. If you turn your head a little bit to the side, sometimes it comes into even better focus. I feel that way about inspiration. You need to know what you are shooting for, and kind of turn to the side, go for a run, take a shower, take a nap, or step back from it a little bit. Talking to people is good, too. I can feel it in my gut. Things need time to incubate. My success tactic is not to only pull it out of the oven, but let it cool.

"It's all spontaneous" is a lot of crap. There has to be a huge amount of work on the front end. The "aha" moment is not a linear progression. You have to develop skill and your talent so when you are doing something else at the beach, like reading a book, or you are in the shower, it feels like "Boom!" This whole new thing, in fact, happened over biological time after developing expertise and talent, and cultivating what it is you think you've got. It *does not* come out of nowhere.

Discover the Creative Edge

FOURSIGHTONLINE.COM

Journal:

- How do you define creativity?
- How do you get unstuck?
- Where does your inspiration come from?

Call to Action:

Do a brain dump right now. For the next ten minutes, write anything that comes to mind without censorship or judgment.

Discover the Creative Edge

BY RAE LUSKIN

Recognize being creative is your birthright,

Adjust, adapt, and change your perspective.

Walk in nature or take a nap,

Encourage wild ideas and wonder.

Engage in childhood fun and play,

Scribble and doodle the day away.

Cultivate a beginner's attitude,

Activate imagination and learn something new.

Define the problem and clear the mind,

Rest in quiet and solitude.

Be observant and ask courageous questions,

Fuel the engine of originality and innovation.

Break through fear, apathy, and inertia,

Discover the power of the creative edge.

CHAPTER THREE

CULTIVATE COURAGE

"Courage is the most important of all the virtues, because without courage you can't practice any other virtue consistently. You can practice any virtue erratically, but nothing consistently without courage."

–MAYA ANGELOU

Our culture is rich with exemplary tales of bravery and self-sacrifice for the greater good. From the cowardly lion in *The Wizard of Oz,* who finds the courage to face the wicked witch in order to save Dorothy, or Neville Longbottom, who tries to stop Harry, Hermione, and Ron from leaving Gryffindor's common room in *Harry Potter and the Sorcerer's Stone.* As Albus Dumbledore says at the end-of-year feast, "There are all kinds of courage . . . It takes a great deal of bravery to stand up to our enemies, but just as much to stand up to our friends."

Courageous leaders have stood up throughout history to fight injustice and oppression—from Susan B. Anthony to Karen Silkwood or Oskar Schindler. They pushed past their fears, took huge risks to make the world a better place for us. Martin Luther King Jr., Gandhi, and Nelson Mandela are the perfect examples of leaders fighting to advance and protect human rights. They faced arrest, intimidation, torture, and even death. Courageous leaders take risks. Entrepreneurs such as Steve Jobs and Walt Disney took financial risks to test the limits of what is possible, and to follow their dreams.

Sometimes courage happens in a moment, and you do the right thing without thinking about it. In 1959 the Dalai Lama denounced the People's Republic and established the nongovernmental Central Tibetan Administration. Rosa Parks refused to sit at the back of the bus. Malala Yousafzai, the Pakistani teen girl, said, "I want an education." The moment you tell your boss his joke is offensive, or you stand up for the person being bullied. It is the moment you say "I don't have the answers," "I need your help," or "I made a mistake." He threatens your child, and you say, "I won't stay in an abusive marriage any longer."

Standing up for someone else is sometimes easier than standing up for ourselves.

Sometimes courage evolves over time. In 1993, I wanted to help victims of childhood sexual abuse, to give them hope and tell them they were not alone. When I wrote my memoir and shared it with some of the respected thought leaders of the time, they said, "Your story is not enough—you need to incorporate other people's stories." Disappointed but determined, I designed a thirteen-page questionnaire, printed it, and mailed it to a number of people I knew who I felt were thriving, and asked them to share the tools that helped them get there. At the time no one was talking about alternative modalities for healing. I theorized art, writing, body work, and spirituality were the keys.

I collected 150 questionnaires and hand-tabulated the results with hash marks (pre computer). The data was rich. I began to write *The Odyssey of Healing: Survivor to Thriver*, but I never got very far. These voices kept saying, "Who do you think you are . . . why would anyone listen to you . . . you are a fraud." You get the idea. So I never wrote the book. I kept all the material tucked away in a file cabinet for twenty years, and for years, I tried to resurrect the project. I wish I could say I finally wrote that book, but I did not; however, other people wrote it. I became a contributing author to Rachel Lev's book *Shine the Light*. After battling my inner demons, I finally did write my first book, and published it in 2010. *Art from My Heart* is a self-discovery journal to nurture self-esteem, resilience healing, and social change using simple art and writing activities.

It takes courage to find your voice and share it with the world. At some point in our lives, we have to face our fears and take a risk: give a speech, quit our job, repair a relationship, face adversity, begin again, be alone, tell our truth, stand up for what we believe is right.

The word "courage" comes from the Latin word *cor*, which means heart. These courageous, ordinary people—like you and me—have the heart to make a difference. They have changed their lives and others' through their willingness to overcome life's challenges, face their fear, and follow their dream.

- Jonny Imerman changed the trajectory of his life to help other cancer patients.

- Debbie Farah combats generations of gender violence in her family and abroad.

- Diane Cranley quit her job to end child sexual abuse.

- Sue Ellen Allen offers hope to inmates in prison.

- Jane Ramsey went to jail to end apartheid.

- Maaria Mozaffar talks about bullying, disrespect, and hatred of women.

"Courage doesn't always roar. Sometimes courage is the quiet voice at the end of the day saying, 'I will try again tomorrow.'"

—MARY ANN RADMACHER—

JONNY IMERMAN

Courage is listening to your own voice—and believing that you can do it.

JONNY IMERMAN WAS A TYPICAL COLLEGE GRADUATE, WORKING IN REAL ESTATE DURING THE DAY AND ATTENDING CLASSES AT NIGHT FOR HIS MBA. JONNY PLAYED BASKETBALL, WORKED OUT AT THE GYM, AND HUNG OUT WITH FRIENDS. AT AGE TWENTY-SIX, HIS LIFE CHANGED.

Jonny was diagnosed with testicular cancer. After doctors surgically removed one of his testicles, he underwent five months of chemotherapy and was declared clear. But almost a year later, four tumors popped up again near his spine, which required another surgery, an eleven-inch incision, and three months of recovery.

Jonny has been cancer-free since 2003. He left the business world behind and began Imerman Angels, a nonprofit organization that connects a person fighting cancer with someone who has beaten the same type of cancer. The mission is to provide a big brother or sister to help inspire and provide tips and knowledge. They have created a global healing community of over four thousand survivors and fifteen hundred caregivers. The service is available *free* to anyone touched by any type of cancer living in sixty countries around the world.

WHAT INSPIRED YOU TO CREATE IMERMAN ANGELS?

I had made a vow to myself during the time I was battling cancer. Each day, every step of the way, my mom was there. My room was filled with family and friends. As I walked down the hall with my chemotherapy IV pole on the way to the bathroom, I saw other people fighting cancer—alone. They were lying in bed, motionless, watching television, or staring in space. It really upset me, and knowing it wasn't right, I started chatting with other cancer patients. I'd say, "Hi, my name is Jonny." We could talk about our emotions, our experiences, things our family couldn't understand, like sucking on lemonhead candy to get the metallic taste out of our mouth.

I wondered: what if every cancer fighter could talk to a cancer survivor who was uniquely familiar with their experience, a person who not only had beaten the same type and stage of cancer, but who also was the same age and gender as the fighter? The cancer survivor would be an angel—walking, living proof that the fighter could win, too. What an amazing connection.

Let's say a nineteen-year-old woman at the University of Richmond gets sick, and she is alone and afraid. She can go on Facebook and talk to an Imerman Angel to find out: What is going to happen to me? How sick will I get? Will I be able to have children? Cancer caregivers, family members, and friends can also benefit from one-on-one connections with other caregivers and survivors.

WHAT ARE THE QUALITIES OF A GREAT LEADER?

Number one, a great leader is focused on a *mission*. He or she believes in the service for the product they're delivering. They believe it in their soul, in every part of their body, and everything about them screams that they get it. They're so fired up to build it, and that's what creates a movement. They have unwavering passion.

WHAT IS YOUR DEFINITION OF SUCCESS?

For me it's simply that we're changing lives—and we're making a difference. I think the most successful people in the world are the people in social enterprise who are building a for-profit company with a social component to make the world a better place, or nonprofits that simply make the world a better place.

WHAT CONTINUES TO DRIVE YOU?

I love people. Everyone's got a story. Everyone has been through challenges. If you talk to somebody for five minutes, you can always learn something from his experiences.

WHAT WOULD YOU SAY TO SOMEBODY WHO SAID THEY DON'T KNOW HOW TO MAKE A DIFFERENCE, BUT WOULD LIKE TO?

You need to dig deep, and think about what has touched your family, maybe diabetes or cancer. Get in touch with one of the groups that serve people in those arenas, and start volunteering. *Be part of the solution.*

HOW WOULD YOU DEFINE COURAGE?

Courage is when you absolutely have no fear of failure. You don't listen to other people who say someone else already had that idea. Ultimately, courage is listening to your own voice and believing that you can do it.

IMERMANANGELS.ORG

Journal:

- What disease or challenge has touched someone close to you?

- What kind of conversations have you had with that person about it?

- Do you talk freely or are you uncomfortable? Why or why not?

Call to Action:

It takes courage to make a difference. Connect with a cause that needs you and touches your heart. Below are several organizations that can help you:

- Points of Light, the world's largest organization dedicated to volunteer service, mobilizes millions of people to take action and change the world. www.pointsoflight.org

- If you are in high school or college, this site will give you a list of seven thousand service learning and volunteer opportunities. www2.ed.gov/students/involve/service/edpicks.jhtml

- Volunteer Match facilitates hundreds of thousands of connections between volunteers and organizations providing community assistance nationwide. www.volunteermatch.org/volunteers/

- WomenOnCall is a unique online network that connects women with specific volunteer opportunities that allow them to share their professional skills with nonprofits. www.womenoncall.org

SUE ELLEN ALLEN

Show up and share your story, even if it's humiliating.

SUE ELLEN ALLEN IS A UNIVERSITY OF TEXAS GRAD AND FORMER EDUCATOR, BUSINESS OWNER, AND COMMUNITY LEADER. HAVING SPENT SEVEN YEARS AS AN INMATE AT ARIZONA STATE PRISON, SHE NOW SERVES AS EXECUTIVE DIRECTOR FOR GINA'S TEAM, AN ORGANIZATION THAT BRINGS EDUCATIONAL PROGRAMS AND SPEAKERS INTO PRISON TO INSPIRE AND EMPOWER INMATES TO STRIVE FOR A BETTER FUTURE. SHE IS ALSO THE AUTHOR OF *THE SLUMBER PARTY FROM HELL.*

In 1994, Sue Ellen and her husband, David Grammer, were indicted by a grand jury and charged with defrauding U.S. investors of around $1.1 million. After pleading not guilty but believing they had little chance of acquittal, they left the country. In 1995 they were tried and convicted in their absence. The fugitive couple lived under false names in Portugal until 2002 when Sue Ellen called the U.S. Embassy in Lisbon and they turned themselves in.

SO HOW DID YOU GET STARTED IN LEADERSHIP?

I had stage-three breast cancer when I entered prison at age fifty-seven. Humiliated and disgraced, I wanted to die. I ended up with a twenty-five-year-old darling cellmate named Gina, from a great family, who was absolutely wonderful. She was sentenced to three-and-a-half years for a $3,000 crime related to drugs. Gina moved in with me to take care of me during chemotherapy because I was so sick. I thought I was going to die—instead, Gina died. Gina collapsed one day, and got sicker and sicker. The medical staff ignored her. Each week she would go back to the infirmary weaker and sicker. They refused to give her a blood test, and she died from myeloid leukemia.

Why did I live when I should have died? Why did Gina die when her whole life was in front of her? I wanted to make sense of that. Prison and Gina's death gave me a new passion and purpose.

Leadership in prison anywhere is not appreciated, it's not recognized, and it's not welcomed. Yet while I was there, I managed to start a cancer walk that is still going on. The first year we raised $10,000 for breast cancer from inmates who make an average of twenty-five cents an hour. Because so many women are touched by breast cancer in family and friends, they were excited to participate. I'm proud to say that walk is now held in every state prison facility for women in Arizona, and has raised over $100,000 for the American Cancer Society. It's a huge event inside. In addition, we started a cancer support group, a Toastmasters club, a life skills course, and the Red Hat Society for the women over fifty. Now some of it took me months and months, even years of begging, but I got it done. You have to keep asking.

WHAT IS THE LEGACY YOU WOULD LIKE TO LEAVE?

In cooperation with Gina's family, we started Gina's Team. We bring volunteer community leaders, speakers, and educators into prisons to teach life skills. Our volunteer programs provide inmates with much-needed tools for re-entry, provide community members as role models, and allow volunteers to see inmates as human beings. It is based on the principles of the ATHENA International Leadership model founded by Martha Mertz: Live Authentically, Learn Constantly, Advocate Fiercely, Act Courageously, Foster Collaboration, Build Relationships, Give Back, and Celebrate. Since 2011, those who attended these classes have an unprecedented recidivism rate of 7 percent. The legacy I seek is bringing hope and light to lives of women behind bars.

WHAT IS THE SECRET TO YOUR SUCCESS?

My big secret of success, which of course is not so secret, is that life is like a minefield, and we are desperately trying to avoid those mines. Nobody wants to blow up, but it's impossible. We can't avoid it. When you try something, sometimes you are going to fail, and you are going to blow up. The key, the secret, is to get back up. Put the pieces back together, and use the experience to help others behind you who are tiptoeing through that horrible minefield. It's about service and helping others with your story. Show up and share your story, even if it's humiliating—that's my secret to a successful life.

HOW DO YOU DEFINE COURAGE?

Courage is different from heroism, or some death-defying act of bravery. Courage is when ordinary people listen to their heart, find their passion, take a risk, and speak up. It's when these same people are willing to be vulnerable and tell their painful story to give hope to others. It's when they experience excruciating loss and pain, and show up anyway. Courage is *never giving up*.

GINASTEAM.ORG

Journal:

- When have you stood up for someone else?

- What is your definition of a hero?

- If you could ask your hero one question, what would it be?

Call to Action:

Find someone you trust and share your minefield story, the story that embarrasses you most. Tell them how scared you are, and ask them to listen without interruption. The first time I did this was at an Overeaters Anonymous meeting. In twelve-step work, in the fourth step, you write out your story, a moral inventory, about every embarrassing and shameful moment. In the fifth step you admit to God, to yourself, and another human being the exact nature of your wrongs. It was really hard. I had thirty pages of stuff I had been holding in, and had been beating myself up about lying as a child, feeling guilty for being fat and embarrassing my children, and wanting a divorce. I had this endless loop running in my head: "You are a horrible human being . . . a fraud . . . you're defective . . . you are disgusting . . . if anyone knew the real you, they would go running for the hills."

I asked a woman whom I had heard speak several times at a meeting to listen to my story. Afterwards she thanked me. She told me how brave I was. I had helped her by sharing my story. She could connect with my humiliation in her own life. It was the beginning of a beautiful friendship.

www.oa.org/newcomers/twelve-steps

DIANE CRANLEY

My life changed on January 18, 2007, when my daughter told me she was being abused by her stepfather.

DIANE CRANLEY IS THE AUTHOR OF *8 WAYS TO CREATE THEIR FATE: PROTECTING THE SEXUAL INNOCENCE OF CHILDREN IN YOUTH-SERVING ORGANIZATIONS* AND THE FOUNDER OF TAALK A 501(C)(3). TAALK STANDS FOR TALK ABOUT ABUSE TO LIBERATE KIDS. DIANE BELIEVES THAT SEXUAL CHILD ABUSE IS PREDICTABLE AND PREVENTABLE WHEN WE SURROUND CHILDREN WITH EDUCATED AND OUTSPOKEN ADULTS. HER LIFE CHANGED ON JANUARY 18, 2007, WHEN HER DAUGHTER TOLD HER SHE WAS BEING ABUSED BY HER STEPFATHER, AND DIANE FINALLY ADMITTED SHE HAD BEEN ABUSED BY A MODELING INSTRUCTOR THIRTY-THREE YEARS EARLIER. THAT WAS THE DAY SHE BEGAN TO SEE HER LIFE'S WORK: A MISSION TO SAVE PAST, PRESENT, AND FUTURE VICTIMS OF CHILD SEXUAL ABUSE, A MISSION TO TOUCH THE LIVES AND CONNECT MILLIONS OF PEOPLE AROUND THE WORLD WHO HAVE BEEN VICTIMIZED AND IMPACTED BY THIS HORRIBLE PANDEMIC. IN THE PAST SIX YEARS, THE TAALK ORGANIZATION HAS SERVED SEVERAL HUNDRED THOUSAND PEOPLE THROUGH ITS PREVENTION AND HEALING PROGRAMS.

HOW DO YOU DEFINE A GREAT LEADER?

The first thing they need to have is integrity. To me, it's one of those things that is not an option. To be a leader, people need to be able to trust that you're going to be honest, tell the truth, and they can have faith in order to let down their guard to follow you. A huge part of that is leading by example, because you know you can't stand up and say one thing—and behave a different way. Transparency is also part of integrity, people being able to see that you walk your walk, or you walk your talk. The bottom line is: we connect from a place of heart, and we're looking to help transform lives, which is true for business as well as the social services. If we're not making a positive impact on people's lives, I think we're off track. People want to follow people who are changing lives and giving hope in some way. Those are the reasons I'd want to follow somebody.

WHAT DO YOU THINK YOUR GREATEST STRENGTH IS AS A LEADER?

Obviously, I look to have all those things we talked about before, like integrity and making a difference in people's lives. The real key for me is my unwavering faith that we can change humanity and transform lives that will have an impact for genera-tions. People often fail to realize that what they do today, every interaction they have, impacts generations to come. Every conversation you have with people not only affects that person, but it affects the way he sees the world, and how he responds to his friends, family, and children.

WHAT OF YOUR LEADERSHIP EXPERIENCE ARE YOU MOST PROUD?

I have to go back to the absolute core because my calling is really from God. I had an experience one night where He asked me to quit my job and commit the rest of my life to serving this epidemic of childhood sexual abuse. The next day I called my boss and took about four months off, and launched the nonprofit. Then I went back to work, but also ran the nonprofit for three-and-a-half years. Now I'm living off of my savings. To me, it's the best example of leading by example. It's tough, and again, not everybody has a calling that is so significant, from a size or commitment perspective.

We all have a calling, but we are stopped by our fears of failure or success, or the feeling you don't have the skills. When our purpose has been revealed to us, we have to put all that fear aside and step out. It's rarely easy. If it is too easy, it probably is not the calling you are seeking. From my perspective, I am an example—you've got to fight through those fears, and follow what you know you're meant to do and be. Because, for me, that's when life opened up. All of the joy flowed into my life when I truly began to do what I know I was put here to do.

HOW DO YOU DEFINE COURAGE?

Courage is when you put yourself in a place to do something hard because you know it is right. Somehow you find the strength and the power deep within to do what needs to be done. When my daughter disclosed her abuse, there was not enough evidence to get a conviction. It took me months working with the police, and be-friending my ex-husband, in order to interact with him so I could get an hour-long recording of him admitting what he did.

TAALK.ORG

Journal:

- Have you ever heard a whisper from the universe?
- What happened when you took a leap of faith?
- What does fear of success mean to you?

Call to Action:

Do you remember the movie *Under the Tuscan Sun*? Diane Lane plays a writer and gourmet cook who, after her divorce, takes a risk and buys an old villa in the spectacular Tuscan countryside. When she begins renovations, a spigot in the front hall is dry. As she rehabs her house, the spigot begins to dribble, and eventually when she is living the life she dreamed of, the water starts to flow freely. She had to take risks to create the life she wanted. At some point we all have to take a risk, even if we are afraid. One of the tools that greatly helped me get to the other side of fear was affirmations. Affirmations are positive statements that describe a desired situation, which are often repeated until they get impressed on the subconscious mind. I believe if you can change your thoughts, you can change your life. I would listen to tapes at night, and in the morning, I wrote out affirmations and repeated them while driving, taking a shower, or walking on the treadmill.

Pick three affirmations and write them on a three-by-five-inch index card. Put one in your pocket, one in your car, and one on your computer. Practice saying them in front of the mirror. Choose from these or write your own:

- I am bold, confident, and courageous.
- I have the courage to step up to any challenge.
- It's natural for me to be brave and take risks.
- I have the courage to follow my dreams.
- Every day, in every way, I am becoming more courageous.
- I have the courage to speak up.
- I feel the fear, and do it anyway.
- I have the courage to look at what needs to be changed in my life.
- I have courage to do the right things at the right time.

DEBBIE FARAH

Courage starts with daring greatly, being transparent, and letting ourselves be seen.

DEBBIE FARAH IS THE CEO AND FOUNDER OF BAJALIA TRADING CO. AND BAJALIA INTERNATIONAL GROUP, FOR-PROFIT AND NONPROFIT COMPANIES, RESPECTIVELY THAT HELP EMPOWER WOMEN AND GIRLS AROUND THE WORLD. SHE DESIGNS AND DEVELOPS COLLECTIONS OF JEWELRY AND HOME AND FASHION ACCESSORIES, WHICH ARE ALL FAIR TRADE AND HANDMADE IN SOME OF THE MOST INCREDIBLE COUNTRIES IN THE WORLD. SHE IS DEDICATED TO FIGHTING POVERTY, HUMAN TRAFFICKING, THE LACK OF EDUCATION FOR WOMEN, AND CHILD MARRIAGES—ALL THROUGH JOB CREATION. THE PRODUCTS ARE SOLD ON HSN, THE SHOPPING CHANNEL, QVC, AND ON THE BAJALIA WEBSITE.

WHAT IS YOUR BACKGROUND?

My mother and father both are from Ramallah, Palestine. My father came at age twenty-seven. My mother came when she was thirteen, and they married in the

United States. My brothers were born first, and I was the third child. Pretty much from the moment I was born, my uncles came into the hospital room and were like, "Why did you do that? Why did you have a girl?" They put my mother down because she had a girl. Girls were not revered in my culture, and were not made to feel special or wonderful. From a very young age I fought that cultural idea and the fact that my brothers got to do and be exposed to things, but I didn't.

In addition, women were not safe. I experienced violence, molestation, and other things from about age ten to fifteen. When it was brought to my parents' attention, they said it was my fault because boys were supposed to do that, and girls were supposed to say, "No." That was a typical Arab answer. Today my mother would say, "We had no idea what we were doing. We were so stupid. We didn't know if this would do damage. We just didn't know." But at the time they were doing what their families had done generations before them. I didn't get any counseling, and thus I carried a lot of pain with me. I also carried a lot of blame and shame throughout my life until I started going through the hard work of healing. Fortunately my creativity has been a great outlet for me. My spirituality has been a great way to help me heal, and reclaim and redefine my life. Working through my history, my past, and my stuff was very courageous.

Because of the childhood abuse, I made some very poor choices, which all had consequences. At age fifteen, I received my first marriage proposal. I was brave enough to imagine a different future for myself. The turning point was at age fourteen when I got my first job. I saw the power of putting money in a woman's hands, starting with me. The job was a way out, and I worked every summer. When I became old enough to go to college, my two brothers were already in college, and my father said he wouldn't pay for my college until one of the boys graduated. This was an excuse, as he never planned to pay for me to go to college. The bank where I worked said, "If you come to work full time, we'll pay for your college." I worked full time and went to school at night in order to do the things I really wanted to do. Every single one of those things made me stronger. The things I overcame made me identify with the women whom I work with around the world. I know their pain, their suffering, and the things they've gone through.

WHAT CONTINUES TO INSPIRE YOU?

A Chinese proverb says, "Give a man a fish and you feed him for a day. Teach a man to fish and you feed him for a lifetime." I say, "Teach a woman to make and sell handicrafts, and you feed her family, strengthen her community, and maybe even change the world." Yes, one generation can change things. Both my mother and grandmother got married at age sixteen. I look at our family now, and both sisters got married, but they were in their twenties. I chose not to marry. One of my nieces is in law school, one's getting her Ph.D. in journalism, and another one finished her master's degree. We are a very different family now than what we were. One of the things that drives me is that one generation can change everything, because we were the generation that changed everything in my family.

A true artist never sees things as they are, but sees things as they can be, and for that reason I remain hopeful. Together we can create a new normal.

WHAT IS COURAGE TO YOU?

The world is a pretty scary place right now for women and children, but it is also a place full of great hope for change. It is the women who stay in the race, get beat up, have their faces scarred, and still continue to speak out. I am courageous when I tell my story. I'm the most courageous when I show up, when I'm present, and when I let people get to know me.

BAJALIA.COM

Journal:

- Where do you find your strength to persevere during tough times?
- What happened when you followed your own heart, versus what your parents expected of you?
- What would you have to do to improve and deepen your relationship with your family?

Call to Action:

Interview members of your family and ask them how things are the same or different from their parents' time.

- Were there expectations based on gender, like "boys don't cry"?
- Was there a double standard? For example, girls should be virgins, and boys should have numerous sexual experiences before marriage.
- How did it impact their life?

Examine your experiences and expectations for your own family. My father did not allow my mother to work. His message was, "You can volunteer." It was a rude awakening for my mom when after her thirty-year marriage crumbled, she had to go to work. When I went to college my father expected me to be a teacher. I refused, and became an art major, which put quite a strain on our relationship. He had a preconceived idea that artists never amount to much. I felt he never understood or respected me until the last few years of his life. I told my daughter, "Be, do anything you want."

JANE RAMSEY

Courage is the willingness to take steps that go against the grain of society.

JANE RAMSEY IS THE PRESIDENT OF JUST VENTURES, LLC, A SOCIAL-JUSTICE CONSULTING FIRM, ACTIVIST, AND LECTURER AT THE UNIVERSITY OF CHICAGO, SCHOOL OF SOCIAL SERVICE ADMINISTRATION. FOR THIRTY YEARS SHE WAS THE DIRECTOR OF THE JEWISH COUNCIL ON URBAN AFFAIRS. IN 2009, *THE FORWARD*, A NATIONAL JEWISH PUBLICATION, PUBLICLY RECOGNIZED HER FOR HER INFLUENCE ON JEWISH SOCIAL JUSTICE. "IN ALMOST EVERY SOCIAL AND ECONOMIC JUSTICE ISSUE THAT CAME UP IN CHICAGO—HOMELESSNESS, UNEMPLOYMENT, COMMUNITY REINVESTMENT, RACISM, ANTI-SEMITISM—RAMSEY WAS THERE, PROVIDING JEWISH LEADERSHIP."

DO YOU HAVE ANY GUIDING PRINCIPLES THAT YOU LIVE BY?

Prophetic Judaism provides a lot of guiding principles in terms of justice, *"Tzedek, Tzedek Tirdof!* Justice, justice shall you seek!" Yes, I think it's critical to have a long view that we're in this, and we don't get discouraged. We need to be able to make progress, and also be aware that we aren't going to get it done. It's not our obligation to finish the task, but it is ours to do what we can to make change.

CAN YOU GIVE ME AN EXAMPLE?

Right after the 9/11 terror attack, we tried to engage in a dialogue with the Muslim community in Chicago. It became harder when we started getting pushback from the mainstream Jewish leadership who said we shouldn't talk to Muslim leaders, and tried to stop us having a relationship with some of the organizations some people had identified as having ties to terrorism. At that point I listened to their concerns, and investigated to make sure we knew who we were talking to before moving forward. We took a lot of heat, but we were compelled by our beliefs, by our understanding, and by a vision of what we could achieve as Muslims and Jews together in creating a better world.

HOW DO YOU DEFINE COURAGE?

Courage is the willingness to take steps that go against the grain of society. You know you're going to get pushed back, and what risks are entailed. Martin Luther King Jr. and Gandhi were beaten up or thrown in jail. But you're compelled to move forward for the greater good.

In 1984 I was a part of a group who decided to sit down at the Consulate of South Africa in Chicago—and not move. At that time, South Africa still practiced apartheid. We were demonstrating weekly against the apartheid, and there was a movement all across the country, and the world, to bring down this horrific policy of institutional discrimination. A group of us allowed ourselves to be arrested for trespassing, and in a jury trial, we were found innocent by reason of the International Law of Necessity. It said we were not liable for our actions because what we were doing was *necessary* to prevent some greater harm.

JUST-VENTURES.COM

Journal:

- What happens to you physically when you are afraid?
- What does it mean to have the courage of your convictions?
- When have you stood up for what you believe?

Call to Action:

Throughout his political career, President Kennedy inspired people to work for the benefit of their communities, their country, and their world. **He believed each person could make a difference, and everyone should try.** The Kennedy family created The Profile in Courage Award in 1989 to honor President John F. Kennedy, and to recognize and celebrate the quality of political courage that he admired most. Study the list of Profiles in Courage Award recipients, or read a biography of someone you admire for their courage.

MAARIA MOZAFFAR

Courage is believing in your heart and your mind and your body you are enough to be victorious in a situation.

MAARIA MOZAFFAR IS PRINCIPAL ATTORNEY AT THE LAW OFFICE OF MAARIA MOZAFFAR. SHE HAS EXPERIENCE IN LEGAL MEDIATIONS, LEGISLATIVE NE-GOTIATIONS, AND POLICY ADVOCACY. SHE SERVED AS LEGAL ADVISOR FOR CAIR-CHICAGO, THE LARGEST MUSLIM CIVIL RIGHTS ORGANIZATION IN THE UNITED STATES. SHE FOUNDED AND CHAIRED THE CIVIL LIBERTIES COALITION OF ILLINOIS. SHE IS THE FOUNDER OF THE SKINLESS PROJECT.

WHAT MAKES A GOOD LEADER?

A leader is someone who understands her or his limitations, but does not accept those limitations. When you want to take charge and try to do something brand new, some people in institutions and organizations will tell you it is not doable—saying you don't have the experience, you don't have the ability, and it's never been done before. A leader will find a way to convince everybody around her this is something that can get done, and something you can do. A leader finds a way to negate the limitation. A leader is persistent.

WHEN HAVE YOU BEEN PERSISTENT?

When I graduated law school I took the bar, and I failed. Then I took the bar two, three, four, and five times, and failed. I even called the president of the bar association, and wrote a long letter sharing my accomplishments and said, "You have to tell me what's wrong here, because I'm doing everything I can. Honestly this test is not reflecting my ability, and the State of Illinois needs me to be licensed." He called and said, "We were impressed with your letter, which we shared with a whole admission's committee, but obviously our hands are tied. I know it's only a few points, but try one more time." I did, and passed.

WHAT IS THE SKINLESS PROJECT?

The Skinless Project is founded on the notion that all women should embrace and cultivate their personal power. This collaborative initiative believes that all women regardless of their age, race, skin color, religion, or financial status deserve the opportunity to be respected for their ideas and personal strength in their communities. We envision a world where a woman is celebrated for her talent, grace, and intellect, which in turn results in her being respected as a powerful leader in her world.

It is a platform to talk about uncomfortable topics. To speak about racism, lack of authenticity, grief, embracing failure, bullying, hate, and disrespect for women. We are tackling negative media and consumer-driven stereotypes, providing global resources, and advocating the undeniable truth: *we are more than skin deep.*

HOW DO YOU DEFINE COURAGE?

Courage is believing in your heart, mind, and body you are enough to be victorious in any situation. Courage is taking a stand when not a lot of people are behind you. Courage is moving forward with self-assurance.

SKINLESSPROJECT.COM

Journal:

- When have you been persistent?
- What stereotypes of women do you see in the media?
- What does "more than skin deep" mean to you?

Call to Action:

Eleanor Roosevelt said, "You must do the thing you think you cannot do."

Find a coach or a mastermind group to support your personal and professional dreams. I traveled the world studying with different people, buying programs and books, and spending tens of thousands of dollars. I was always searching, waiting for the magic pill that would fix me. My teachers have been some of the premier personal development and expressive arts leaders, including Mary Morrissey, Janet and Chris Attwood, Marci Shimoff, Lisa Nichols, Jack Canfield, Judith Cornell, Daria Halprin, and Julia Cameron, to name a few. I heavily invested in myself with numerous coaches and several yearlong mastermind groups with Steve Harrison and Lisa Sasevich, and now with Felicia Searcy.

What I finally realized is *I'm not broken*. The answers are inside of me. No one person can make me better. A coach or mentor, however, offers support, learning opportunities, tools and techniques, structure and accountability. Build your confidence. Invest in yourself. If you are interested in a free twenty-minute consultation, contact me at rae@thewinningadventure.com.

Risk

—AUTHOR UNKNOWN

To laugh is to risk appearing the fool.

To weep is to risk appearing sentimental.

To reach out to others is to risk involvement.

To expose feelings is to risk exposing your true self.

To place your ideas, your dreams, before a crowd is to risk their loss.

To love is to risk not being loved in return.

To live is to risk dying.

To hope is to risk despair.

To try is to rIsk failure.

But risks must be taken, because the greatest hazard in life is to do nothing.

The person who risks nothing, does nothing, has nothing, and is nothing.

They may avoid suffering and sorrow, but they cannot learn, feel, change, grow, love, or live.

Chained by their attitudes, they are slaves; they forfeited their freedom.

Only the person who risks can be free.

CHAPTER FOUR

CONNECT AND COLLABORATE FOR SUCCESS

"Alone we can do so little; together we can do so much."
–HELEN KELLER

Leadership and collaborations intrigue me. I have been on boards since I was twenty-three, and in numerous coalitions at various stages of their development. I've held different positions, from worker bee to president. Eleven years ago I joined with several women under Jewish Women International to start J-Cares (Jewish Community Abuse Response Education and Solution) in response to a Jewish woman being killed from domestic violence in the Chicago area. It was clear to me from the beginning that we needed to expand our vision to include abuse across the lifeline of a woman, from childhood sexual abuse to rape, domestic violence, and elder abuse. I lobbied hard for that, and at times, I was the disruptive voice. During strategic planning, I might suggest instead of worrying where the funding is coming from, let us imagine a world where our organization was no longer needed. As we have evolved over the years, our vision has expanded, and the coalition now consists of over fifty services providers, community partners, and advocates.

Creative activism is inherently a collaborative process. In the development of this book, I interviewed over 120 leaders around the country. I specifically asked how they encourage people to step up and lead, as well as how they engaged people in their vision. Six approaches stood out:

1. Be authentic and genuine in your interactions. When you share personal stories of challenges and failures, you build trust.

2. Foster a climate of mutual respect by listening to their stories and learning from them.

3. Encourage and support learning and personal growth. Help everyone to live her or his purpose.

4. Create a culture that encourages people to ask for help, and take risks even if things don't go well. When people have permission to fail, they will think outside the box.

5. Align everyone around a set of values and a shared dream.

6. Share the credit with your team, sponsors, or clients.

Learn more from these master collaborators.

- Dr. Melissa Gilliam works with academics, gamers, storytellers, and teens to create games that improve reproductive health.

- William Karesh, D.V.M., collaborates on the intersections of wildlife and health in remote parts of the world.

- Paul Schmitz is an advocate for youth empowerment and diversity who uses his personal story to build rapport with future community organizers.

- Matthew Zachary, a thirty-nine-year-old cancer survivor and pianist, has valuable advice on how to educate and empower young cancer patients.

- Jonny Boucher, a twenty-six-year-old musician, partners with mental health organizations and musicians on suicide prevention in schools.

- Tom Walter, an award-winning entrepreneur, created a values-based company with high employee engagement, and went from "good to great."

"Individual commitment to a group effort-that is what makes a team work, a company work, a society work, a civilization work."

—VINCE LOMBARDI—

DR. MELISSA GILLIAM

*Everyone brings a piece
of the puzzle together.*

DR. MELISSA GILLIAM IS A PROFESSOR OF OBSTETRICS AND GYNECOLOGY AND PEDIATRICS, CHIEF OF THE SECTION OF FAMILY PLANNING AND CONTRACEPTIVE RESEARCH, AND ASSOCIATE DEAN FOR DIVERSITY AND INCLUSION IN THE BIOLOGICAL SCIENCES DIVISION AT THE UNIVERSITY OF CHICAGO. SHE CREATED THE CENTER FOR INTERDISCIPLINARY INQUIRY AND INNOVATION IN SEXUAL AND REPRODUCTIVE HEALTH (CI3) TO FACILITATE COLLABORATIVE RESEARCH AND PROGRAMMING, AND TO LEVERAGE THE UNIVERSITY'S RESOURCES TO MAKE SIGNIFICANT IMPROVEMENTS IN THE SEXUAL AND REPRODUCTIVE HEALTH OF VULNERABLE COMMUNITIES.

DR. GILLIAM CO-FOUNDED THE GAME CHANGER CHICAGO DESIGN LAB (GCC), AN INITIATIVE IN WHICH YOUTH COLLABORATE WITH FACULTY AND UNIVERSITY STUDENTS TO CREATE DIGITAL STORIES AND GAMES IN ORDER TO EXPLORE HEALTH AND SOCIAL ISSUES. GCC PROGRAMS AND WORKSHOPS HELP YOUTH HONE SKILLS IN MEDIA LITERACY, CRITICAL INQUIRY, STORYTELLING TECHNIQUES, AND GAME DESIGN.

WHAT CAN YOU TELL ME ABOUT YOUR WORK?

A huge part of what I do is working directly with youth. We started a series of projects where we are combining sexual reproductive health, social health, and emotional health with storytelling. If you teach people how to tell a story and talk about themselves, not only is it very compelling for them, but it's also fascinating for people to hear. I work primarily with urban youth of color to empower them and show them that their life stories are captivating to people. In addition, we add digital media and technology in the form of games called Transmedia. The games actually are linear or story-based games that incorporate multiple forms of media. The games can be very low-tech, only involving paper and pencil, or it can be more high tech, where we're working with youth developing videos, websites, and other projects.

HOW DO YOU COLLABORATE?

We have run a series of workshops that focus on collaboration and leadership. These include faculty and professors from our team, graduate students, undergraduates, and then high school students. We work together with an idea for a week or two. Everybody's bringing a piece of the puzzle together. No one alone could do the project. We work in a very integrated kind of free-flowing prototyping, showing and sharing, getting feedback and trying again.

For example, we designed a card game about reproductive health. We set aside a week to work in our center space. The team consisted of four youth, four graduate students, two faculty, and two staff members. The objective: when people play, they will explore in more depth issues like sexually transmitted infections (STI). It will impart a certain amount of knowledge because you need to know what this is and how to treat it, but we also talk about the social and emotional implications of STIs. We wanted to talk about communication, stigma, and resilience, all the things that youth deal with on a personal level related to STIs. We didn't want to only medicalize it, we also wanted youth to be thinking about the role this is playing in their lives, and in their communities.

With a broad range of specialists in health, game design, and graphics—and four youth with no expertise—we started playing a variety of games, modifying them so we could clearly understand the mechanics of games. We told stories, talked about how you tell stories, and we talked about sexually transmitted diseases. We answered their questions and showed them how we use computers to research, find, and pull in health knowledge.

We started mocking up prototypes, some using index cards and dice, while others came up with board games. We critiqued them and gave feedback, thought about problems, and solved them. By Thursday of that week, we decided on how our game would work, and then worked on the logistics, the balance, and other factors. There would be moments when we'd all say, "Well, how is that going to work?" And, "I don't like this, we're not reaching that goal," and "We wanted communication, and we wanted this, and let's take this person's game." At times the group process would break down, and we'd have to figure out how to rebuild it, but it worked. By the end we had a playable, fun, and functioning game. In post-production right now, we're smoothing it out, making sure we have all the pieces, sending it to experts to make sure our facts are correct and it is age appropriate. Next we'll do another prototype, create a series of cards, introduce it to a classroom where we will study and assess knowledge and understanding.

CI3.UCHICAGO.EDU

Journal:

- What kinds of games do you like to play?
- How do you brainstorm a new idea?
- Who do you include in your process?

Call to Action:

Create a board game with your family or friends. Imagine a game of life. Consider the following areas: health and wellness, loving relationships, rewarding work, creative expression, adventure and fun, service and making a contribution, financial freedom, personal and spiritual growth. What does that look like to you? Pay attention to the process and how you work together. Does one person take the lead? How do you arrive at the vision for the game? How do you decide on the rules?

SMS

DR. WILLIAM KARESH

I don't need to convince you that my vision of the future is better than your vision of the future. We just have to find a mutual benefit.

DR. WILLIAM KARESH IS THE EXECUTIVE VICE PRESIDENT FOR HEALTH AND POLICY AT ECOHEALTH ALLIANCE. HE HAS PIONEERED INITIATIVES IN DOZENS OF COUNTRIES, FOCUSING ATTENTION AND RESOURCES ON SOLVING PROBLEMS CREATED BY THE INTERACTIONS AMONG WILDLIFE, PEOPLE, AND THEIR ANIMALS. HE COINED THE TERM "ONE WORLD–ONE HEALTH" TO DESCRIBE THESE INITIATIVES, WHICH LINK PUBLIC HEALTH, AGRICULTURE, AND ENVIRONMENTAL HEALTH ORGANIZATIONS AT BOTH LOCAL AND INTERNATIONAL SCALES. HE HAS AUTHORED OVER 150 SCIENTIFIC PAPERS AND NUMEROUS BOOK CHAPTERS.

TELL ME A BIT ABOUT YOUR BACKGROUND.

In the early sixties, I was fascinated with *Wild Kingdom* on television, and brought home a lot of wounded animals. I wanted to be a professional working with animals, but my family was not encouraging. They wanted me to be a doctor or a lawyer. In college I found myself switching from one major to another, from economics to business to engineering, and finally art. I did not care about any of them. A friend of my mother's convinced me to switch to biology because I loved working with animals. When I did, a light went on. At school I found a mentor in the zoology-biology department who took me under his wing, and for the first time I got a four-point average. Animal conservation work made me happy. I learned early on when people say, "No, you can't do something," don't be dissuaded; find another way to get to where you want to be, or another way to make something happen. It's made me feel successful, certainly in my career, to be able to do and make things happen where others didn't think it was possible.

HOW DO YOU GET STAKEHOLDERS ENGAGED IN YOUR VISION?

It's like being at an art reception, walking up to somebody and introducing yourself. In our line of work, you have to identify who are the key stakeholders, and if you are working in the Congo, it's very apparent you need to talk with the local villagers and hunters. A local hunter might not understand the Ebola virus as an emerging infectious disease, but he knows where gorillas spend the day. A villager might not care about gorilla conservation, but as you talk to them, you find they don't like their children getting sick—or dying. Then I can say we have a solution that will protect your children and protect gorillas too, if we work together.

If we're going to be successful in preventing disease, we have to talk directly with the people, and find out what concerns them. It is vital to identify the ways we can help each other achieve possibly different things and come out ahead. I don't need to convince you that my vision of the future is better than your vision of the future. You care about health, and I care about saving animals, and working together we both achieve our goals.

HOW DO YOU GET YOUR STAFF TO STEP UP AND LEAD?

Pay attention to what their skills and abilities are. Look at their interests and temperament. Push people to do more than they think they can do, if you think they can do it. I encourage people to try new things, and I want people to try things and fail a little, because failure is a good thing.

As I said before, it is important to mentor and nurture people. It is important to recognize that their vision may not be mine, and to encourage them to follow their dream. For instance, Lisa, whom I have worked with for several years, wants to be a yoga instructor. I have two choices: let her go, or give her the time off in the afternoon to take classes. She has a different goal in life, but she can still help me in the morning by being incredibly productive in making our program successful. We don't have to have the same goal in life with the same vision.

ECOHEALTHALLIANCE.ORG

Journal:

- How does the work you do today reflect what you enjoyed as a child?
- How do you engage people at home or at work to step up and lead?
- When have you been successful in empowering others?

Call to Action:

I love to mentor young people and be a sounding board for them. They are so interesting and dynamic, and their curiosity and inquisitiveness delight me. One young woman I met at the health food store was struggling, trying to figure out who she was in the world. I offered to let her move in with me for three months while she figured out her life. As I mentored her, I received so many gifts. She was a raw vegan. I had never heard of raw, and she showed me how to make the most delectable raw pie and influenced my later wellness plans. Mentoring works both ways. A great mentor can mean the difference between failure and success.

Be a mentor for Big Brothers Big Sisters of America, the oldest and largest youth mentoring organization. **bbbs.org**

WHAT IS A MENTOR?

- Mentors are guides there to help their mentees find life direction, but never to push them.

- Mentors give insights about keeping on task, and setting goals and priorities.

- Mentors are authentic, and share their own life experiences.

- Mentors use failure as teachable moments.

- Mentors are sounding boards.

- Mentors provide constructive feedback.

- Mentors motivate by setting a good example.

- Mentors want their mentees to succeed.

PAUL SCHMITZ

I believe that understanding and sharing our personal stories, how we have formed our beliefs, values, and experiences, is important to leading.

PAUL SCHMITZ IS THE SENIOR ADVISOR AT COLLECTIVE IMPACT FORUM. HE FOUNDED PUBLIC ALLIES MILWAUKEE IN 1993 AND SERVED AS CEO OF PUBLIC ALLIES FROM FEBRUARY 2000 TO AUGUST 2014. PROFILED BY *MILWAUKEE MAGAZINE* AS "A TIRELESS ADVOCATE FOR YOUTH EMPOWERMENT AND DIVERSITY," PAUL WRITES AND SPEAKS OFTEN ON TOPICS OF NATIONAL SERVICE, CIVIC ENGAGEMENT, COMMUNITY BUILDING, DIVERSITY, LEADERSHIP, NONPROFIT WORKFORCE DEVELOPMENT, AND SOCIAL ENTREPRENEURSHIP. PAUL IS CO-FOUNDER AND CHAIR OF THE NONPROFIT WORKFORCE COALITION, COCHAIR OF VOICES FOR NATIONAL SERVICE, A FACULTY MEMBER OF THE ASSET-BASED COMMUNITY DEVELOPMENT INSTITUTE AT NORTHWESTERN UNIVERSITY, AND A BOARD MEMBER OF THE UW–MILWAUKEE HELEN BADER INSTITUTE FOR NONPROFIT MANAGEMENT. HE'S THE AUTHOR OF *EVERYONE LEADS: BUILDING LEADERSHIP FROM THE COMMUNITY UP.*

WHAT IS THE MISSION OF PUBLIC ALLIES?

Our mission is to advance leadership in order to strengthen communities, nonprofits, and civic participation. We want to bring new, diverse leadership, age eighteen to thirty-five, to the table, working together as cocreators to develop community capacity to solve problems effectively and sustainably. We believe that:

1. Everyone can lead. Leadership is an action many can take, not a position that only a few can hold.

2. It is about taking personal and social responsibility to work with others on common goals. Everyone has some circle of influence where it is possible to take responsibility for leading.

3. It is the practice of values that engage diverse groups to work together effectively; the means are as important as the ends.

Let me share a story with you. My children and I went to see the Pixar movie *Ratatouille*. In the film a rat named Remy dreams of being a chef. He goes to Paris to follow his dream, and allies himself with an errand boy, Alfredo Linguini, hiding in his hat, and guiding him to become a master chef. The film has both drama and comedy, but in the end the truth is revealed and the critic, Anton Ego, declares Remy the greatest chef. "Not everyone can become a great artist, but a great artist can come from anywhere." At Public Allies we realize that great leadership can emerge from uncommon places.

HOW DO YOU INSPIRE PEOPLE?

When I travel around the country meeting with Allies members, I am being fully authentic and open about my life and challenges, admitting my mistakes, sharing a list of things at which I suck. This opens a door for people to see me not as Big Boss Man, but as a human being. They see someone who struggles like they do, and who doesn't expect perfection. I share my story because so many young people think that leadership means never being vulnerable—and that showing weakness is bad.

WHAT IS YOUR STORY?

Growing up in a middle-class Catholic family in Wisconsin, I was the youngest of six siblings. I never felt like I measured up at home or in school, did not fit in with the engineers or the athletes in my family. To compensate for my low self-esteem, I became rebellious, a smart aleck, and a bully. I began drinking in elementary school, and started taking and dealing drugs in high school. I landed in treatment. From my time in treatment and recovery among a diverse group of people, I gained the value of recognizing and mobilizing assets. Until then, I had not realized all the prejudice I carried around race and sexual orientation, for example. I began questioning my beliefs, and I realized how much I had in common with everyone and I was in no position to judge.

WHAT HAPPENS AFTER YOU SHARE YOUR STORY?

After my talk, I give them an opportunity to ask questions, as well as challenge and explore their own lives. One of the activities we do is called Life Maps, where they use words and images to describe the major events in their lives that brought them to their values and purpose. Everyone gets to present his or her life map. This tool establishes a foundation for people to understand each other, and not make assumptions. At the end of the exercise, people feel they can connect with everyone in the room, and this starts to build a sense of community. Giving them authentic learning experiences motivates and helps them believe. If I can make a difference, so can you.

EVERYONELEADS.ORG

Journal:

- What people, events, or experiences have had the greatest impact on your life?
- What judgments do you make about people by the way they look?
- What lessons have you learned from listening to other people's stories?

Call to Action:

Create Life Maps with your team. Gather some magazines, scissors, glue sticks, colored pencils, or pens and paper. Spend thirty-five minutes to an hour on this activity.

1. Write down the important events of your life. Consider when and where it happened, as well as how you felt about it.

2. Determine which pictures will represent those events. You can sketch them or look for them in magazines.

3. On a blank piece of paper, put them in chronological order, starting with your birth on the left corner, and the present on the upper right.

4. Glue them down, and share your story.

5. An alternate version would be to bring in photos of you at different ages and write a story about each one.

MATTHEW ZACHARY

I have used social media to make Stupid Cancer the largest nonprofit of its kind in the United States.

MATTHEW ZACHARY WAS A TWENTY-ONE-YEAR-OLD COLLEGE SENIOR AND CONCERT PIANIST EN ROUTE TO FILM SCHOOL WHEN HE LOST USE OF HIS LEFT HAND. HE WAS DIAGNOSED WITH PEDIATRIC BRAIN CANCER. EIGHTEEN YEARS LATER, HE IS AN AWARD-WINNING RECORDING ARTIST. HIS FIRST TWO ALBUMS, *SCRIBBLINGS* AND *...EVERY STEP OF THE WAY*, HAVE BEEN DISTRIBUTED TO MANY CANCER CENTERS AND NONPROFIT ORGANIZATIONS BECAUSE OF THEIR SOOTHING AND GENTLE NATURE.

A FOUNDING MEMBER OF THE ORIGINAL GOOGLE HEALTH ADVISORY COUNCIL, HE LAUNCHED STUPID CANCER IN 2007. AS CEO OF STUPID CANCER, A 501(C)(3), MATTHEW HAS BUILT AN EXTRAORDINARY TEAM OF STAFF MEMBERS AND VOLUNTEERS WHO HAVE HELPED LAUNCH A SOCIAL MOVEMENT, UNITING SEVERAL INDUSTRIES TO ADDRESS THE UNDERSERVED NEEDS OF YOUNG ADULTS AFFECTED BY CANCER.

WHY ARE YOU FOCUSING ON YOUNG-ADULT CANCER?

Every eight minutes a young adult is diagnosed with cancer. *This is not okay*. This neglected group has limited resources, inadequate support, and, more importantly, a lack of awareness and understanding from the community around them.

They have unique needs that other age groups do not, such as fertility, dating, sexuality, parenting, insurance, financial assistance and career planning, education, and peer support. Young adults with cancer are faced with isolation, and the medical community is grossly uneducated on how to effectively communicate about diagnosis, treatment, and support.

When I got my diagnosis, I was given six months to live and was told if I survived, I would never play the piano again. When I did live, I had no direction, and had to start over in the advertising field. It took me six years to meet another person who had gone through what I did. The Internet was in its infancy, and we had very little support. My family and I had to go it on our own and hope for the best. What gave me the final push to start a charity was a report in 2006 that young-adult survival rates *had not improved in thirty years*.

I founded Steps for Living, which became I'm Too Young for This! Cancer Foundation in 2007 and rebranded in 2012 as Stupid Cancer, which I thought would appeal to millennials because it's what Homer Simpson would say. Our organization seeks to empower young cancer survivors through music, cancer advocacy, consumer health marketing, and technology.

WHY DO YOU THINK YOU HAVE BEEN SUCCESSFUL?

I have focused on innovation, enterprise strategies, community wealth, and brand partnerships. I have used social media to make Stupid Cancer the largest nonprofit of its kind in the United States. We have a hip and edgy lifestyle brand for our youth cultures and have millions of subscribers, friends, fans, readers, listeners, and members. We forged alliances with national public health institutions and young-adult advocacy organizations. We launched the Internet's premiere online young-adult resource community, produced more than a dozen young-adult cancer conferences each year, and innovated social media and mobile health platforms for improved patient outcomes. We connected thousands of cancer centers to our resources, and socially mobilized millions to a progressive new movement that is demanding change from an establishment that so far has ignored them.

In addition, we do real research to prove that we are making a difference. In collaboration with David Victorson, an associate professor of medical social sciences at Northwestern University, and the founder of the young-adult cancer support organization, True North Treks, we conducted a survey of 120 individuals, including survivors and caregivers, before and after they attended the 2013 Stupid Cancer Conference. The survey sought to measure levels of social connection, confidence, and knowledge about young-adult cancer survivors. They reported a 24 percent increase in feeling more connected to other young-adult cancer survivors, a 15 percent increase in their knowledge about young-adult cancer issues, and a 29 percent increase in their access to young-adult cancer resources after the conference.

Similarly, caregivers surveyed reported a 17 percent increase in knowledge on young-adult cancer issues, and an 11 percent increase in their access to young-adult cancer resources after the conference.

STUPIDCANCER.ORG

Journal:

- What kind of data have you collected to support your cause?
- How does your brand help you forge alliances and partnerships?
- How have you used social media to promote your organization or cause?

Call to Action:

Giving money to your favorite cause or organization is very fulfilling. Knowing how your dollars are contributing to a community, and making a difference in people's lives, requires some research. Analyze how well a charity is doing before you make a donation.

In 2007, Charity Navigator recommended using these criteria when considering making a donation. **charitynavigator.org**

1. Able to communicate who they are and what they do

2. Has defined short-term and long-term goals

3. Able to state the progress it has made (or is making) toward its goal

4. Implementing programs that make sense to the donor

5. Appears trustworthy

6. Feel you can make a long-term commitment

JONNY BOUCHER

Never underestimate the conversation that you're having with someone because you could be talking to your next best friend, or your biggest supporter or investor.

JONNY BOUCHER IS THE FOUNDER OF HOPE FOR THE DAY. A MUSICIAN, HE RAN THE GAMUT OF JOBS IN THE MUSIC INDUSTRY, FROM BOOKING SHOWS TO TOURING IN BANDS. HE STARTED HOPE FOR THE DAY IN 2010 AFTER HE GOT THE NEWS THAT HIS BOSS, MIKE, A MAN WHOM HE IDOLIZED, HAD KILLED HIM- SELF. JONNY KNEW THE IMPACT OF SUICIDE PERSONALLY, BECAUSE HIS FRIEND MARK, A DRUMMER, WHOSE FAILED ATTEMPT TO SHOOT AND KILL HIMSELF IN 2004, LEFT HIM BLIND. JONNY KNEW HE *HAD TO* DO SOMETHING. HE TURNED HIS LOVE FOR MUSIC INTO A MOVEMENT THAT CHAMPIONS MUSIC AND ARTS AS AN ALTERNATIVE TO SUICIDE. HOPE FOR THE DAY HAS REACHED THOU- SANDS BY PROVIDING OUTREACH AT CONCERTS, FESTIVALS, AND COMMUNITY EVENTS, WHERE THEY TALK ONE-ON-ONE TO THOSE WHO TAKE AN INTEREST AND PROVIDE THEM WITH RECOVERY INFORMATION AND RESOURCES.

HOW DOES HOPE FOR THE DAY WORK?

Hope for the Day utilizes music and the arts as an alternative approach to handling suicide and mental illness. We are all about empowering those who feel that they're not worthy. I want kids to know that when they're feeling down and out, as musicians, they can use their guitars, or take a pen and a pad and write down lyrics. Growing up, I had all this music equipment, with a guitar riff going on a loop pedal. I would get behind my drum set and go on for days, releasing the emotional struggles and energy I had in my body that needed to be gone.

In 2013 we partnered with Alternative Press to bring *The Music Saved My Life* video series that features internationally recognized musicians and artists who share their personal stories of struggling with suicide, depression, and mental illness. They share their creativity, and how music is a pathway to recovery. When you hear someone's story, it allows you to relate to them and the music you already love more deeply because you know the person who wrote it was going through the same stuff you're going through. So . . . maybe there is a way that I can get through this.

Another initiative we have is called BEATKEEPERS, a creative education program focusing on empowering urban youth through musical and artistic expression. We work with at-risk adolescents, sixteen- to twenty-one-year-olds, from low-income areas of Chicago who are coping with mental illness. BEATKEEPERS inspires these youth to confront suicide, community issues, and oppression through lyric composition and beat making. It encourages them to take responsibility in their communities. They learn team building, and become inspiring members of the community.

HOW DO YOU INSPIRE PEOPLE TO STEP UP AND LEAD?

When I got my job with Mike, we met for drinks. He asked me where I was from and what I do to establish some common ground. Next he asked me, "What are your flaws?" I said, "Oh, I don't know, sometimes I get discouraged, and I back myself down from doing what I know I can actually do." We started talking about personal flaws, and he shared he liked to drink, and he said he would never pass judgment against me for anything I would do in my personal life, as long as I used good judgment on the job. Right now I am the only person running the show, and I rely on interns. I invite them for coffee in a public place, which seems to take away their anxiety—and I have the same conversations with them that Mike had with me.

WHO ARE YOUR COLLABORATIVE PARTNERS?

I am on the board for Mental Health America of Illinois, MHAI, the longest-running mental health organization in America. One day I walked into their office unannounced, and said, "My name is Jon Boucher, and I just started this nonprofit organization to reach out to at-risk youth utilizing music and art. I figure you guys are a big deal, and we should talk to see how we can work together." They gave me a huge honor to be a coach for their board because I am the youngest person on that board. It's fun to walk into a room, wearing T-shirts, jeans, and my tattoos, because everyone knows that I'm "the kid." We are trying to get more people from the medical world and the entertainment world to financially invest in the organization so we can start going on more tours and reaching more kids.

When we're out talking with the youth, I hit them with honest and tangible real-life experiences they can relate to—whether it be Mark or Mike's story. People can relate because they've had people in their lives who have gone through hard times, and all you can do is be there for them. Since I have joined the board, I also advocate for the American Foundation for Suicide Prevention. They love who I am because I'm willing to knock on doors, I'm willing to go out there because I don't care if I talk to five thousand kids—or one. I am willing to have conversations with anyone. I can bring hip-hop to the South Side, or I can take punk rock to a predominantly white neighborhood. I have learned never underestimate the conversation that you're having with someone because you can be talking to your next best friend, or your biggest supporter or investor. You may never talk to that person again, but your conversation might leave something with them that will travel and connect with them.

HFTD.ORG

Journal:

- How do you establish rapport with people when you first meet them?
- What are your strengths and what are your flaws?
- What do your clothes and style say about you to other people?

Call to Action:

Create a list of potential partners, sponsors, donors, and investors. Look on LinkedIn, and try to connect with them. Offer to take them to coffee. Recently I spent a half hour with Marc J. Lane, an expert in social enterprises, who teaches social enterprise at Northwestern University School of Law. We had been friends on LinkedIn for many years, but we never met. I asked him about the benefits of becoming a social enterprise, and he gave me a lot of food for thought. Part of my dream is to start creative activist clubs in the workplace, in colleges and high schools. Marc suggested there might by intellectual property involved, and a possible source of revenue. When I left, he said he would love to support me in an upcoming Creative Activist Retreats or a Google hangout, and gave me a copy of his newest book, *The Mission-Driven Venture*.

People want to help you if you ask.

Best-selling author Steven Pressfield identifies the primary stumbling block to creating as resistance. It often takes the form of procrastination, so put a time and a date on your calendar, and start making appointments. Tell yourself you are going to make three to five calls a day. Be persistent, because sometimes it takes several calls to connect.

TOM WALTER

Every member of the company has their say, but not necessarily their way.

TOM WALTER, CHIEF CULTURE OFFICER OF TASTY CATERING COMPANY AND A SERIAL ENTREPRENEUR, IS A NATIONALLY RECOGNIZED SPEAKER ON ENTRE-PRENEURSHIP, LEADERSHIP, AND BUSINESS CULTURE. HE HAS BEEN AN OWN-ER/OPERATOR IN THE FOOD AND BEVERAGE SERVICE INDUSTRY FOR OVER FORTY YEARS. TOM HAS STARTED TWENTY-NINE COMPANIES AND ACQUIRED THREE. TOM SERVES ON THE ADVISORY BOARDS OF FIVE CHICAGO-AREA COM-PANIES AND TWO UNIVERSITIES. IN ADDITION, HE IS AN ACTIVE MEMBER OF THE ACADEMY OF MANAGEMENT AND THE SMALL GIANTS COMMUNITY. HE IS A MEMBER OF THE CHICAGO ENTREPRENEURSHIP HALL OF FAME. HE FOCUSES ON THE IMPORTANCE OF HUMAN CAPITAL, VALUES-DRIVEN ORGANIZATIONAL CULTURE, AND HIGH SERVICE STANDARDS. AS A RESULT, TASTY CATERING HAS WON NUMEROUS AWARDS FOR EXCELLENCE IN CULTURE AND IN CATERING, SUCH AS A "BEST PLACE TO WORK" AND "CATERER OF THE YEAR."

HOW DO YOU EMPOWER PEOPLE?

I'm focused on their personal lives, their professional lives, furthering their careers, and providing lifelong learning. Our companies run in such a way that we are focused on a culture. I'm also focused on their families, so our mantra is first comes God or your Higher Power, followed by your family, education, and work.

HOW DID THAT EVOLVE FOR YOU?

In 2005 two young leaders, who had worked for me since they were teens, said, "If you don't change, we're leaving." We had just bought a huge building and exploded our business. I couldn't afford to lose them, as one of them was the CFO, and he was only twenty-five, and the other at age twenty-four was our logistics director. They said, "We don't like command and control. We don't like being given orders, we don't like management, and we want a culture-driven leadership." I had about ten seconds to either decide yes or no. I looked at them, saying, "I don't know how to do it, but I will support you."

HOW WERE YOU ABLE TO CREATE SUCH CHANGE?

They bought Jim Collin's book, *Good to Great,* for everybody in the company because it came in Spanish and English. They established teams instead of silos. Eight people from different teams who we thought had the highest moral and ethical fiber sat in our conference room, and determined the core values and culture statement. They filled the white board with all sorts of core values, listing forty or fifty. The first one they agreed upon is: we will always be moral, ethical, and legal. The second one is: we'll treat all with respect. The third is education. They proceeded to identify seven core values, and went back to their teams where everybody agreed to it. We have the values posted everywhere, and before any meeting with three or more people, we recite the culture statement. Sometimes I say them five times a day.

WHAT OTHER CHANGES HAVE YOU MADE?

We all eat lunch together as a family from 12:30 to 1:00. They see all the metrics because the profit-and-loss statement, our core values, and culture statement are all posted on the wall. When we challenge each other, we call out the core value.

The Good to Great Council meets the third Monday of every month for two hours. Each team sends a representative so everybody can be heard. There is a predetermined agenda so the key points and the factors of the business are covered, such as employee engagement, disruptors within the organization, strategic and tactical changes, brand marketing, and communications. The first half is a predetermined agenda; the second half is spent on current tactical or operational concerns. The decisions are posted throughout the company or by email because every member of the company has their say, but not necessarily their way. They understand that their voice was heard, and their peers made the decisions. They have always made the right decisions, which included foregoing bonuses during the recession, and volunteer wage reductions.

Transparency is critical. Communication is critical. We write a company newsletter called "Inside the Dish." We have a template in a Word document, and every team contributes. What is amazing—they put in praise and appreciation for each other. The corporate sales team will thank the culinary department for last-minute orders.

TASTYCATERING.COM

Journal:

- What style of leadership is in place at your organization?
- What kind of leader are you?
- How transparent is your organization?

Call to Action:

Henry Ford said, "If everyone is moving forward together, then success takes care of itself." People join organizations or work at companies for a number of reasons. I know I joined National Council of Jewish Women because a friend asked me to help out with the Silent Witnesses when she was going out of town. I respected this woman, and I loved the mission of this organization: to improve the lives of women and children. When I was fifty, I was president, and was pretty much the youngster of the group. I hired our first paid employee, and we designed a short survey and did small focus groups. We wanted to know why people joined in the past and what younger women were looking for in an organization. The younger women wanted one-time or short-term volunteer opportunities. Most of them were working and had limited time. They were also looking for support/programing around raising Jewish children. We created programs that fit their needs and still honored our core values, and the next generation grew.

Take a short survey of members of your organization. Ask a few pointed questions:

- How did you hear about the group?
- Why did you join this organization?
- If a person asked you to join, what did she say?
- What are the benefits of being part of this group?
- Why do you stay?

Heart of Collaboration

RAE LUSKIN

Imagine magnificent, meaningful relationships
Dare to openly express your thoughts and feelings
Declare boldly rejoicing, I walk my talk
The heart of collaboration.

Develop the art of the extraordinary in others
Recognize their contributions in public and private
A thoughtful remark, a word of encouragement
The heart of collaboration.

Find a mentor and build a support network
Ask for help, insight, and guidance
Let go of ownership and share the credit
The heart of collaboration.

Live a legacy of commitment and contribution
Be the torchbearer who ignites a special spark in others
Create something of enduring value and pay it forward
Be the heart of change and collaboration.

CHAPTER 5

DREAM A BETTER WORLD

"Whatever you can do or dream you can,
begin it. Boldness has genius, and magic
and power in it. Begin it now."

–GOETHE

A vision begins with a dream in your heart, then a picture in your mind. It is something imagined you would like to make real for your life. Ideas turn into intentions and a desire to make something happen. A vision is the expression of your desire for a future that is better in some important way than what exists for you now. Imagine waking up each morning enjoying every moment, feeling fulfilled and free, and having the courage and confidence to change the world.

Having a clearly detailed vision is essential to global transformation. The light bulb profoundly changed human existence by illuminating the night. The electric light, one of the everyday conveniences that we take for granted today, was invented in 1879 by Thomas Alva Edison. He was neither the first nor the only person trying to invent an incandescent light bulb, but he made it better and cheaper. He held this vision: to make electricity so cheap that only the rich will burn candles.

Consider the vision of the Apollo moon project: to place a man on the moon by 1969. This clear vision and directive from President Kennedy in 1961 generated and focused an incredible amount of energy. When they began the project, the technology did not exist. However, they overcame insurmountable obstacles, and on July 21, 1969, Neil Armstrong stepped onto the moon's surface.

Now it is time for you to tap into your courage and genius and unleash your unbridled imagination. Envision you have a magic wand and you can do anything. You have the power to change lives and communities. Ask yourself: what is the best way for me to serve and make a significant contribution to making the world a better place?

DEFINE, DECLARE, AND COMMIT.

A vision is more than pages written in your journal or the goals you set forward for the next three years. It is a breathing, living document that pulls back the curtain on your longing. When you get clear on what it is in your heart, what you really want, it will give you confidence during bad days and keep you from losing your motivation when things are going well. With clarity of purpose comes the ability to center your attention and efforts on your goals, with less distraction and doubt. It will override decisions that you might make out of fear. Knowing your purpose, and having an audacious vision, will enable you to encourage others. An inspired vision will help you become the brightest, most magnificent expression of yourself. When you dream big, you will move beyond limitations, and go from where you are to where you want to be.

Everybody's vision or message is unique and will evolve. Your desire to add value, give to others, create something, and express yourself may be smaller and more personal in the beginning, and grow larger and expand over time, like these creative activists.

- Katherine Josten started with a $1,500 loan twenty years ago to create a multicultural celebration of peace through art.

- Shannon Galpin, a mountain biker, had a dream to empower women in the conflict zone of Afghanistan.

- Social justice educator Paul Kivel had a desire to make the world a safer place, where everyone has a voice at the table.

- Actress Naomi Ackerman teaches children about healthy relationships through theater, and gives a voice to victims of domestic violence.

- Mary Rockwood Lane brought healing art into health care.

- damali ayo wants to create a new model of activism through love and courage, rather than fear.

"Whatever the mind can conceive and believe, it can achieve."

—NAPOLEON HILL—

KATHERINE JOSTEN

*The idea is as simple as it is profound,
to create world peace through art.*

KATHERINE JOSTEN IS AN ARTIST, EDUCATOR, SPEAKER, AND FOUNDER/DI-RECTOR OF THE GLOBAL ART PROJECT FOR PEACE, A MULTICULTURAL CELE-BRATION OF PEACE AND DIVERSITY THAT HAS ACTIVELY INVOLVED 130,000 PARTICIPANTS IN EIGHTY-SEVEN COUNTRIES ON SEVEN CONTINENTS. SHE WAS NOMINATED FOR THE 2002 UNESCO PEACE PRIZE FOR TOLERANCE AND NON-VIOLENCE. HER WORK INSPIRES PERSONAL AND SOCIAL EVOLUTION THROUGH CREATIVITY.

I WAS A PAINTER AND AN EDUCATOR WITH AN MFA, TEACHING AT THE COLLEGE LEVEL FOR TWELVE YEARS. IN 1991 I HAD THIS IDEA FOR THE GLOBAL ART PROJ-ECT THAT WOULD ALLOW ME TO TOUCH MORE TEACHERS AND PEOPLE, VERSUS ME HAVING ONE EXHIBITION OR TEACHING ONE CLASS. I BORROWED $1,500 FROM MY PARENTS TO START THIS THING TWENTY YEARS AGO. I HAD NO COM-PUTER, NO CONTRACTS. PEOPLE TOLD ME YOU CAN'T MAKE THIS WORK. BUT I WOULD GO INSIDE MY MIND AND VISUALIZE THE RIGHT PERSON OR RESOURCE THAT I NEEDED. ONE THING LED TO THE NEXT THING.

HOW DOES THE GLOBAL ART PROJECT WORK?

Participants create a work of art every two years in any medium, expressing their vision of global peace and goodwill. The art is displayed locally in each participant's community. Global Art Project then organizes an international exchange by matching participants, group-to-group and individual-to-individual. The exchange occurs April 23–30, resulting in thousands of people sending messages of peace around the world at one time, and visions of unity simultaneously encircle the Earth. The art is sent as a gift of global friendship and is exhibited in the receiving community.

WHAT IS THE MISSION OF THE GLOBAL ART PROJECT?

The mission of the Global Art Project is to joyously create a culture of peace through art. The project celebrates multiculturalism and diversity. The larger mission is to teach that we are all one. We don't have to be afraid of things, thoughts, or people that are different than us. In addition, we can all make a difference and take actions that promote a worldwide community of peace, love, and friendship.

WHAT DO YOU MEAN WHEN YOU SAY THE GLOBAL ART PROJECT IS HEALING?

You need to go inside and generate a feeling of peace before you can create art that expresses peace. You can't create it in physical reality if you can't visualize it. The art you create is a personal, unconditional gift of love you are sending to a stranger. Also, community organizers and teachers get to create the art and facilitate dialogues about peace issues. The global cooperative exchange participants experience numerous visions of peace, little ripples spreading out into the world. So it is healing for the individual, the community, and the world.

WHAT ARE SOME OF YOUR FAVORITE PIECES?

Several images come to mind, like the eight-year-old girl who created an artwork with the earth, the sun, moon, angels, insects, including all beings on earth. One of my favorite was a fifth-grade Japanese student who drew an astronaut with his arm around some weird creature, with earth in the background. One woman sent cookies in the shape of the earth, plus the recipe. Some have written books and poems, while others created CDs of their music. Schools have created wall murals, and they document the process and final pictures.

WHAT IS YOUR VISION FOR THE GLOBAL ART PROJECT GOING FORWARD?

I see the Global Art Project being the ying counterpart to the yang of the Olympics. What I mean by that is the Olympics are every four years, but really every two with the summer and winter Olympics, and the Global Art Project is every two years. The Olympics is about physical excellence, whereas the Global Art Project is aesthetic or metaphysical. The Olympics are about competition, whereas the Global Art Project is about cooperation. The Olympics are exclusive, and only the best can participate, whereas the Global Art Project seeks to be inclusive. Anyone, anywhere can participate.

I want a Global Art Project peace museum. I'm now on the advisory board of the International Network of Museums for Peace, and I know exactly what I want it to look like. The first floor is going to be gallery space so we can have exhibitions of the art created for peace. Part of the Global Art Project is "Let's all join hands," and we've got thousands of these paper hands for peace. I want to have a permanent exhibition of those hands, thousands of them hanging from the ceiling where people can walk around them. Also on the first floor is the market with products for sale. We're sitting on these incredible visions of peace that need to be on calendars, note cards, and aprons in order to inspire people. Besides the gallery space, there would be a small theater space where visitors can go see images of people from around the world who have participated with their art, as well as art from around the world to inspire people. On the second floor would be the administrative offices of the Global Art Project. On the property we would also have some casitas/studio space where teachers can bring their students and create art. Here regional directors can conduct workshops and collaborate.

GLOBALARTPROJECT.ORG

Journal:

- What does "celebrate diversity" mean to you?
- When have you been afraid of an idea or a person that was different?
- How have you contributed to creating more peace in the world?

Call to Action:

How different our lives would be if world leaders and everyday people could sit down and explore how we can move toward peace. It seems so outside of ourselves, yet revered leaders such as Gandhi, Aung San Suu Kyi, Martin Luther King Jr., and Nelson Mandela all explored other approaches to conflict.

The Dalai Lama has said, "We must commit ourselves to living peacefully, with kindness, generosity, and compassion. The quality of our lives, the joy, and our happiness rests in our ability to experience internal peace in any situation."

Viktor E. Frankel, a holocaust survivor, said, "Everything can be taken from a man but one thing: the last of the human freedoms, to choose one's attitude in any given set of circumstances, to choose one's own way."

Peace begins with you.

Take the next few moments. Sit comfortably, close your eyes, and breathe. Listen to the sound of your breath going in and out while relaxing your head and shoulders. Notice this deep sense of calm pouring into every part of your body. In your mind's eye, see a candle burning. Notice the colors of the flame, the golden outer edge, and the blue center flare. See the bright light pouring into your heart, becoming brighter and brighter, filling your whole body with a soft golden hue. Feel this love bubbling up inside of you. Imagine you are in your home, and it is filled with your family and friends celebrating. Hug everyone and say hello, and send them the light. Each person begins to glow. They vibrate this energy of love, compassion, gratitude, and forgiveness. It keeps growing and expanding as they leave and go into their lives and community. You know it is a friendly universe basking in harmony and joy. Now, return your attention to your body and your breath, wiggle your toes and fingers, and move your head from side to side. Keep in your heart this vision of peace. Write or draw how you feel.

SHANNON GALPIN

One woman can make a difference, but an army of women could change the world.

SHANNON GALPIN, 2012 *NATIONAL GEOGRAPHIC* ADVENTURER OF THE YEAR, IS BEST KNOWN FOR FOUNDING THE NONPROFIT MOUNTAIN2MOUNTAIN IN NOVEMBER 2006. THE AUTHOR OF *MOUNTAIN TO MOUNTAIN*, SHE DEVELOPED EVENTS THAT INVOLVED COMMUNITIES AND PROVOKED DISCUSSION THROUGH ART, MUSIC, AND SPORT. SUPPORTING GRAFFITI ART PROJECTS AND CREATING THE STREETS OF AFGHANISTAN EXHIBITION, SHANNON HAS FOCUSED ON PROJECTS THAT EMPOWER THE VOICE OF WOMEN IN CONFLICT ZONES AND INSPIRE OTHERS TO COMBAT APATHY. AN AVID MOUNTAIN BIKER, SHE CONTINUALLY FOCUSED ON BREAKING GENDER BARRIERS. IN 2009, SHE BECAME THE FIRST WOMAN TO MOUNTAIN BIKE IN AFGHANISTAN, A COUNTRY WHERE WOMEN ARE NOT ALLOWED TO RIDE. SHE IS CURRENTLY PRODUCING A DOCUMENTARY FILM ABOUT THE AFGHAN WOMEN'S CYCLING TEAM.

WHAT INSPIRED YOUR WORK IN AFGHANISTAN?

When I was pregnant with my daughter, I received a call saying my sister had been raped in college. I had been raped ten years before, and I knew as I was driving to the hospital to be with my sister that the world needed to change—and I needed to be part of it. Having a unique insight into gender violence, and becoming a mother, I knew I wanted to create a safer, better world for women. Pretty much overnight I decided to start a nonprofit to learn about "the ingredients" that create violence and oppression of women. If I was going to truly study gender violence, I needed to go to Afghanistan, ranked the worst place in the world to be a woman.

WHAT ARE SOME THINGS YOU HAVE LEARNED OVER YOUR NINETEEN VISITS?

One of the things that moved me most was visiting Kandahar prison. I was overwhelmed by the outpouring of stories from the women—certainly a turning point for me. They were desperate to be heard, to know that their injustice, struggle, and heartbreak would survive outside the prison walls. Their voices mattered, and owning your own story is the core of who we are. If we don't use our voice, how do we create change? That became the thread of all the work I started doing with Mountain2Mountain, whether it was in the arts, or with athletes.

HOW DID YOU GET INVOLVED WITH BIKING THERE?

In 2009, I first took my bike there. It was an experiment of sorts to test gender barriers that prevented women from riding bikes. As a mountain biker, I was very excited to explore Afghanistan. I wanted to see what people's reactions would be. Would they be curious? Would they be angry? Would I have a better insight into why women can't ride bikes there? It's one of the few countries in the world where that's still a taboo. The bike became an incredible icebreaker. I used it to spark conversation with people I met along the way, asking the men if they would ever allow their daughter or wife to ride. Most men said no; they considered it immoral.

Eventually, in 2012, I met a young man who was part of the men's national cycling team. They invited me to go for a ride with the men's team, and I met the coach, who I learned was also coaching a women's team. He started it because his daughter had wanted to ride, and as a cyclist, he thought this is something girls and boys should be able to do. I met with the women's team. Dressed in long pants and full sleeves, with their headscarves tucked beneath their helmets, they practiced before dawn on the highways, using poor-quality equipment. I pledged to provide equipment for the team and support races and continued coaching to hopefully spread it to other provinces. Unfortunately things are slow to change; the women are still insulted, and people continue to throw rocks. This culture has never supported women. For example, very few women drive in Afghanistan, and the few that do get the same reaction. Men do not want women to be independent and free, and cars and bikes represent that. These women are incredibly brave, because they are literally on the front line of changing their culture.

WHAT IS YOUR VISION FOR THE FUTURE?

Going forward, our focus is built around our Strength in Numbers program. The backbone of Strength in Numbers is the belief that one woman can make a difference, but an army of women could change the world. Bikes have long been a symbol of freedom of mobility, and a tool of the women's suffrage movement in America in the early 1900s. We used bikes to unify the women we work with to pedal a revolution of change for women's rights here and elsewhere in order to make it a better place for women and girls around the world.

Some of our key initiatives are:

- Expand the women's cycling movement outside of Kabul.

- Petition their involvement in the 2016 Olympics in Brazil as observers.

- Focus on team development for future racing/possible exchange outside of Afghanistan to gain a spot for the 2020 Olympics in Tokyo.

- Plan for a Women's Summit and solidarity ride.

- Initiate one-week mountain biking camps in the United States for women who have survived gender violence, or girls at risk, to empower them to become leaders in the fight for women's rights globally.

SHANNONGALPIN.COM

Journal:

- What is the story you have been wanting to tell?
- When have you contributed or participated in a solidarity event?
- What volunteer activities have made you feel so engaged you couldn't wait to come back again and help out?

Call to Action:

Pick a cause and walk, ride, or run to show your support. One of the most profound experiences I had was participating in a march in Washington, D.C., with the Silent Witnesses Initiative in October 1997. This project was started by artist and writer Janet Hagberg in order to commemorate the lives of twenty-six women killed from domestic violence in Minnesota in 1990. There were life-size red wooden figures with a gold shield on the chest that told how each woman was murdered. It became a springboard and a catalyst for victims to come forward and bring media attention to leaders in Congress. The National Council of Jewish Women adopted this project in Illinois, and we had a contingency go to D.C. At that march, over fifteen hundred advocates and volunteers from all fifty states walked from the Washington Monument to the Capitol steps. Then we laid out the figures around the reflecting pond. It looked like a cemetery. It was a powerful visual reminder that one in four women experience domestic violence in her lifetime. I felt so proud to be there, to be part of something bigger than myself.

PAUL KIVEL

What I would like to see is a multicultural society based on love, caring, justice, and interdependence with all living things.

PAUL KIVEL, A SOCIAL JUSTICE EDUCATOR, ACTIVIST, AND WRITER, HAS BEEN AN INNOVATIVE LEADER IN VIOLENCE PREVENTION FOR MORE THAN THIRTY-FIVE YEARS. HE IS AN ACCOMPLISHED TRAINER AND SPEAKER ON MEN'S ISSUES, RACISM AND DIVERSITY, CHALLENGES OF YOUTH, TEEN DATING, FAMILY VIOLENCE, RAISING BOYS TO MANHOOD, AND THE IMPACT OF CLASS AND POWER ON DAILY LIFE. PAUL IS THE AUTHOR OF NUMEROUS BOOKS, INCLUDING *UPROOTING RACISM: HOW WHITE PEOPLE CAN WORK FOR RACIAL JUSTICE*, WHICH WON THE 1996 GUSTAVUS MYERS AWARD FOR BEST BOOK ON HUMAN RIGHTS; *MEN'S WORK: MAKING THE PEACE; HELPING TEENS STOP VIOLENCE, BUILD COMMUNITY AND STAND FOR JUSTICE; BOYS WILL BE MEN: I CAN MAKE MY WORLD A SAFER PLACE*: AND MOST RECENTLY, *YOU CALL THIS A DEMOCRACY? WHO BENEFITS, WHO PAYS, AND WHO REALLY DECIDES.*

HOW DO YOU INSPIRE THE STAKEHOLDERS AROUND YOUR PURPOSE?

In our society, people are very fragmented, segregated, individuated, and yet we all have tremendous needs to come together in community for support, sharing, and vision. First, people need to recognize themselves as community, to share their stories and visions—to discover their common purposes and their common needs, and begin to identify what they might do together. It involves holding a safe space for other people to step forward and facilitate conversation. It's not about having a common purpose in mind, and trying to win people over to it. So often social justice work is focused around a conversion narrative. We have a campaign that we want other people to be excited about, or to recognize the importance of, and so we try to convince them, in various healthy or unhealthy ways, that they should join us. We fail to understand that people are already in community, they already have needs and visions, and it's our job to strengthen their ability to come together collectively and make a difference.

WHAT KIND OF TOOLS DO YOU USE TO HELP THEM COME UP WITH THEIR VISION?

We allow people to step back from the harsh reality of their daily lives and truly imagine the world they want to live in, not the world they do live in. We ask them to consider:

- What would they like to see?

- What kind of relationships would they want to have?

- What kind of institutions would they want to live within?

- What would things look like visually?

- What would they feel like?

- What would be different about their lives, and the lives of their children?

You can do that with art. You can do it with discussions. You can do it with visualizations. There are different modalities for creating a more relaxed, intuitive, and imaginative space for people. It's also about sharing that, either working on things collectively, or doing some individual work, and then finally coming together and sharing these things collectively.

DO YOU HAVE A FAVORITE MODALITY?

I like drawing, because it's not something a lot of people do all the time. It's a powerful tool, especially breaking into small groups and having people draw together, and beginning the process of collectively creating some visual image of what they'd like to see.

HOW DO YOU GET PEOPLE TO STEP UP AND LEAD?

Many times people don't see themselves as a leader, because they think if they are not leading a movement of ten thousand people in the streets, they're not truly a leader. So it's helping them realize, in fact, in lots of situations they've intervened or became involved, or supported or provided leadership of some sort, and therefore, *this is* something they can do. A famous quote from a Jewish rabbi is, "It's not upon you to finish the task, but neither are you free to desist from it." Basically, each of us has a role to play, and we're not going to save the world, any of us individually, but we each have something we can do, a contribution we can make. What I want people to get in touch with is the way they can step up and make their contribution.

HOW DO YOU DO THAT?

I encourage people to start where they are. We are all in relationships. We talk to people at work and in the community. We don't want to marginalize anyone. The phrase I use to keep me mindful of this is: "Nobody left out, nobody left behind." Who's being left out? Who's being left behind? Who's not at the table?

We're making choices all the time to either build community or to stay separate and weaken the community where we would like to be a part. It is helping people understand that they know how to do it, to be a little bit stronger and bolder about reaching out, intervening, stepping up, and making a difference.

WHAT IS YOUR VISION?

I envision a society where each person is valued, regardless of gender, race, cultural background, sexual identity, ability or disability, or access to wealth. This society would provide adequate shelter, food, education, recreation, health care, security, and well-paying jobs for all. The land would be respected and sustained, and justice and equal opportunity would prevail. Such a society would value cooperation over competition, community development over individual achievement, democratic participation over hierarchy and control, and interdependence over either dependence or independence.

I would like to see a multicultural society based on love, caring, justice, and interdependence with all living things.

WWW.PAULKIVEL.COM

Journal:

- What is your definition of a great community leader?
- What are your strengths as a leader?
- Who is not at the table in your discussions?

Call to Action:

Write your vision for world transformation. I am very good at seeing the big picture. It is one of my best skillsets. I have a three-year, one-year, and six-month vision. I have included a portion of my vision, which I read or write twice a day. The year is 2017. I am grateful my work is so rewarding. I know the message of the creative activist has taken hold. There have been living room conversations and park bench discussions about how one person can change the world. There are more stories on television and radio highlighting the good work of people around the world. We now live in a world of good news. The missive is we are all connected. Diversity is respected and embraced. Education is a creative mecca. People are stepping up to the plate with unique and innovative programs and campaigns to create world peace and a sustainable planet. There are more collaborations between artists, community, and business leaders. Conversations are more inclusive. We are blessed to live in a time where so many are committed to making a loving, peaceful, equal, respectful, and safe world for women and children. Everyone is encouraged to dream big, live on purpose, and be unstoppable.

Theater has the power to give voice to the silent and be a voice of change.

NAOMI ACKERMAN IS AN ACTRESS, STILT WALKER, AND PROFESSIONAL CLOWN. NAOMI WORKS AS A FREELANCE CONSULTANT TO ORGANIZATIONS AND SCHOOLS, ADAPTING AND CREATING DRAMA TECHNIQUES TO DEAL WITH IDENTITY, GENDER, AND SOCIAL-JUSTICE ISSUES. SHE IS A SOCIAL ACTIVIST, MEDIATOR, AND CONFLICT-RESOLUTION SPECIALIST. NAOMI HAS WORKED FOR THE PAST TWO DECADES USING ART TO PROMOTE PEACE AND CHANGE AND ENCOURAGE SELF-EMPOWERMENT. SHE WAS ONE OF THE FOUNDING MEMBERS OF VIEW POINTS, AN ARAB-JEWISH THEATER GROUP PROMOTING TOLERANCE AND DIALOGUE, SPONSORED AND PRODUCED BY THE PERES CENTER FOR PEACE. SHE IS FOUNDER AND DIRECTOR OF THE ADVOT PROJECT, A REGISTERED 501(C)(3) THAT USES THEATER TO FACILITATE SOCIAL CHANGE.

WHY DID YOU BECOME AN ACTIVIST?

I wanted to use the stage to create a world where kindness prevails. Theater has the power to give voice to the silent, and be a voice of change. I came to activism naturally; my parents lived social activism. They raised me to care because it is the right thing to do.

I was commissioned by the Israeli Ministry of Welfare to write a monologue about battered women called "Flowers Aren't Enough." It is a universal story of power and control, and of someone losing who she is because someone put her down. I interviewed women in a shelter in Jerusalem, and I wrote this intimate twenty-minute piece, it evolved over time, and it's now fifty-five minutes. Those women's stories inspire me. Against all odds, they rise up. There is a need for this story, and I have performed it over eighteen hundred times globally, and it has been translated to Arabic and Spanish, and is being performed in the Middle East and Spain. I have been called the Queen of Domestic Violence because I am the voice of those who have been hurt, and I am the voice of those who cannot speak for themselves. In March 2004, I performed "Flowers Aren't Enough" at the United Nations in honor of International Women's day, in front of the Commission for the Status of Women.

WHAT ARE YOU WORKING ON NOW?

Since that time, I was moved to found Advot, which means "ripples" in Hebrew, because like a ripple, kindness, love, and change start small and grow. Our mission is to use theater as a tool to promote social justice, raise awareness, and facilitate social activism. We foster self-esteem, promote healthy relationships, and prevent violence through interactive drama experiences. Theater companies tell stories, but few use theater as a tool for social change.

Currently we are implementing our program, Relationships 101. This unique curriculum consists of a series of workshops that deal with dating abuse and healthy relationships. The program focuses on teens, ages fourteen to eighteen. Relationships 101 targets self-advocacy through effective communication skills. There is a very big need for learning how to be in relationship, and how to communicate face-to-face. Everything is through email, FaceTime, and texting, and we have forgotten how to look someone in the eye and say hi.

More important, it strives to help teens understand that they can advocate for themselves, and they can influence the environment around them. We use theater as a way to practice and rehearse for real-life experiences. Once you try something, and you are "acting" out a better choice, you are more confident. Our program ends with a final dramatic presentation written and performed by the participants. It is being implemented in public schools, private schools, summer camps, and the boys/girls juvenile probation detention camps in California.

TELL ME ABOUT YOUR WORK WITH INCARCERATED YOUTH.

Last year I was given unprecedented permission to film my program in the juvenile detention facility where I work, and where cameras are never allowed. People are very interested. It is like peeping through a little hole that nobody ever gets to go through. I am telling a different story. Usually we hear only about the tragedies of their lives. But I want to talk about the possibilities of change. These are children, so there is laughter and fun. Sure, they are in jail, and they have had horrible lives. But they have their whole life ahead of them, which they can change so things are different. I want to show the world, and ask for their help. I am in the process of raising funds to produce "The Captive Audience."

WHAT IS A SOCIAL ACTIVIST?

In your everyday life, you are doing your best to be actively mindful of the people around you, and your own community. We don't need to teach people to be social activists, but we need them to be actively social in their life—certainly a paradigm shift to "be my brother's keeper," to be responsible for another's welfare. One day I brought chips to the young people in jail, and they were ecstatic. It's the little things, it's an intention, and it is sometimes as simple as a bag of chips. It is our job to figure out someone's chips, give them their favorite, and make them smile.

THEADVOTPROJECT.ORG

Journal:

- How do you feel about texting and email as a primary form of communication?
- When was the last time you looked somebody in the eye and said hello?
- How can you be your brother's keeper?

Call to Action:

Plan a good-deed day at home, work, or in the community. Put into practice the simple idea that every single person can do something to improve the lives of others and positively change the world. In 2009, President Barack Obama signed the Edward M. Kennedy Serve America Act. He said, "We need your service, right now, at this moment in history. I'm not going to tell you what your role should be; that's up to you to discover. But I am asking you to stand up and play your part." One of his goals was for middle and high school students to do fifty hours of community service per year.

WHAT IF WE ALL DID THAT?

Create a service project based on what interests you. Imagine how good you will feel as you develop your talents and abilities, leadership and organizational skills. You will gain confidence and your self-esteem will soar. It might even change the direction of your life.

Nine steps to a successful service project:

1. Decide on a subject that really interests you or has a personal connection.

2. Research what is currently being done in your community.

3. Create a vision for your proposed project: include current resources, time, money, energy, and the people who can support your project.

4. Connect and collaborate with sponsors and partners.

5. Delegate work.

6. Get permission.

7. Advertise: create a flyer or press release; use social media.

8. Celebrate your accomplishments.

9. Measure and evaluate: What did you learn? What did you accomplish? What would you do differently? How could you improve upon it?

For more information on good-deed days, visit gdd.goodnet.org/about.

MARY ROCKWOOD LANE

Be visionary. Go inward into your own visions and bring them out to change the world.

MARY ROCKWOOD LANE, PH.D., RN, IS THE COFOUNDER AND DIRECTOR EMER-ITUS OF SHANDS ARTS IN MEDICINE PROGRAM AT UNIVERSITY OF FLORIDA-GAINESVILLE, WHERE SHE CREATED THE FIRST ARTIST-IN-RESIDENCE PROGRAM OF ITS TYPE IN THE UNITED STATES. AT A TIME WHEN ART WAS NOT INTEGRAT-ED IN HEALTH CARE, MARY BECAME INSPIRED BY HER EXPERIENCE OF HEALING HERSELF THROUGH ART—AND SHE CREATED A PROGRAM THAT INCORPORATES ART, MUSIC, POETRY, THEATER, AND DANCE INTO THE MEDICAL PROFESSION. SHE DIRECTED THE NATIONALLY RECOGNIZED ARTS IN MEDICINE PROGRAM FOR OVER FIFTEEN YEARS. TODAY SHE WORKS TO PROMOTE A VISION FOR A MORE CREATIVE AND TRANSFORMATIVE NURSING PRACTICE.

MARY, COULD YOU TELL ME YOUR STORY?

I was a young mother with two young children when my husband left me—and I crashed. My support network was ripped away, and everything shattered. A deep sense of despair and rage took over. Therapy wasn't working, and my therapist said I needed to try something different. I had so many fears about not being good enough, but I was willing to try something new. It was almost as if a part of me rose out of the ashes, like the phoenix rising. I had this incredible opportunity of recreating my life.

I had never made art before, but I decided I was going to be an artist. I went to a studio and selected a canvas, picked up a brush, and began to paint. I became immersed in the process of painting, the way the colors, textures, and the different shapes swirled together on the canvas. I forgot about how I felt, and instead painted those feelings of pain and anger. My despair became a series of self-portraits, which were all distorted with garish backgrounds, and they were crying and bleeding. When I finished releasing the image onto canvas, I stepped back and *gasped*. What I saw was an aspect of myself that I couldn't face. It was so ugly, I backed away, left the studio, and went home. Later I realized I had left behind the pain and the past—and I *was free*.

WHAT INSPIRED ARTS IN MEDICINE?

I read *Re-Enchantment of Art* by Suzi Gablik, where she called to artists to step out of their studios and go out and change the world. To paraphrase: "Art is a necessity in life, not a luxury. We need to fuse it in every part of our life." A lightbulb went off, and I said, "Of course, we need to bring artists into the schools, we need to have artists in the streets, we need to have artists in the hospitals, we need to bring in the arts, and not only the artist but the artist within us. We need to invite this artist within us to come forth in ourselves to really be everything we can be."

The artist represents an ancient healing energy in our culture that we had not been utilizing enough, and it could change the world.

WHY DO YOU THINK YOU WERE A SUCCESSFUL LEADER?

From my personal experience and passion, I had embodied this vision that art was healing. As a nurse working in a hospital, in partnership with a physician, I was able to use all the resources of my life to bring change into the health care system. People around me sensed my passion, this fire in me, and artists in the community caught on fire, and with this clear vision, we were all committed to manifest this dream. We are going to work at the bedside with patients, we're going to meet with the executive directors, the CEOs, nursing managers and nurses, we're going to talk about what we want to do, and get feedback, whether they choose to be involved or not. We wanted to invite feedback on what's working and what's not working, and gain the trust as a group in order to begin bringing the arts to the bedsides of patients.

HOW DO YOU GATHER STAKEHOLDERS AROUND A COMMON PURPOSE?

Share your vision with people. One of the things we did when we started the arts and medicine program was to invite all kinds of groups: businesses, community, church groups, the vet school, social workers. Never underestimate the power of speaking and sharing to gain support for the work you're doing, because if it resonates with people, it's almost like an energetic field that ripples out into the pond. This openness, inviting people to be part of the vision, gives them permission to make it their own.

The veterinary school is a perfect example. We were asked to speak there, and I remember thinking this is funny, why would they be interested in art for healing? We shared the dream of what we wanted to do. It surprised us when they began to share how they would integrate art for healing with people who were grieving for their animals.

You don't always know where your words will settle, and you don't need to.

MARYROCKWOODLANE.COM

Journal:

- What is a deeply meaningful, creative experience you can share with others?

- What book or movie has inspired you?

- Who can you collaborate with on your vision?

Call to Action:

Create a plan with S.M.A.R.T. goals: Specific, Measurable, Attainable, Realistic, and Timely.

Answer the following questions:

- Who: Who is involved?

- What: What do I want to accomplish?

- Where: Identify a location.

- When: Establish a time frame.

- Which: Identify requirements and constraints.

- Why: Specific reasons, purpose, or benefits of accomplishing the goal.

We have to conquer fear and work from a place of love.

DAMALI AYO IS A SPEAKER, AUTHOR, RADIO ESSAYIST, AND ARTIST. SHE IS THE AUTHOR OF TWO BOOKS, *HOW TO RENT A NEGRO* AND *OBAMISTAN*, PLAYFUL YET BITING SATIRICAL EXAMINATIONS OF RACE RELATIONS. HER WRITING, ART, AND LECTURES HAVE ENGAGED TOPICS RANGING FROM RACE, GENDER, SEXUAL ASSAULT, AND SEXUAL ORIENTATION TO SPIRITUALITY, CHRONIC ILLNESS, THE CREATIVE PROCESS, HEALING, MUSIC, AND TRASH. HER WORK HAS BEEN FEATURED IN PUBLICATIONS WORLDWIDE, INCLUDING *HARPERS*, *THE VILLAGE VOICE*, SALON.COM, *THE WASHINGTON POST*, *SEATTLE TIMES*, *CHICAGO TRIBUNE*, *REDBOOK MAGAZINE*, *THE O'REILLY FACTOR*, AND BOOK TV.

HOW DID YOU GET STARTED IN CREATIVE ACTIVISM?

When I attended Brown University, I studied politics and American culture. While there I started working in theater and performance. Through the Women's Prison Project, I taught, designed, and directed theater workshops for inmates at the Rhode Island women's prison. This program is still running today, and has inspired several other programs of its kind across the country. Though I have always been a creative person, after college I thought I would be a writer. However, when I had a dream about a visual art collage that would powerfully describe one of my many experiences with racism in middle school, I turned to art. In 2003 I created the web-based art-performance work rent-a-negro.com. A pioneer in this web-based art, my website received four hundred thousand hits per day the first month, as well as global media attention. It was a satirical website that examined racism. The premise—that you could rent a black person for your personal entertainment—led to my first book, *How to Rent a Negro*, a satirical commentary on contemporary race relationships. For many years, I focused my stories to help find ways to end racism. These days I have broadened my work to include stories from all parts of my life and experience, opening my heart and my life to help people find the courage to face their lives with love, and live to tell their own stories.

WHY DO YOU THINK YOUR PRESENTATIONS ARE SO WELL RECEIVED?

When I share a story with an audience, something shifts; they get a new perspective, and they don't feel alone when laughter is shared. People thrive when their inner world is mirrored by someone who articulates their struggles while being affirmative, positive, and transmitting a sense of hope. This is what I do.

WHEN YOU GET STUCK, HOW DO YOU GET UNSTUCK?

I have a cup of tea and watch a lot of documentaries, or I will listen to interviews of other creative people not in my field. I'm currently watching a documentary on the heavy-metal band Metallica. I love to take baths and listen to classical music or Bruce Springsteen. I realized this last year I had to give myself space to feel my feelings. I've been writing a book about femininity, and one of the biggest pieces was learning how to feel again. Too often I simply barrel through something, just going through the motions, so I had to learn to sit still, feel this or feel that.

WHAT IS YOUR VISION GOING FORWARD?

I want to see a new approach to activism and social change. We have to conquer fear, and work from a place of love. I am invested in making this shift in our culture. My presentations, and the way I share my experience, honor the whole human being. I share stories about how we think, how we feel, how we learn, how we fight, how we love, how we fight for what we love, and most of all, how we are transformed. I want people to meet themselves and latch onto hope, affirmation, and a positive way forward into the future that we create *not alone, but together.*

DAMALIAYO.COM

Journal:

- What movie mirrored a struggle you were encountering?
- How did it help you?
- What happens to you when you go through the motions without feeling them?

Call to Action:

We all get stuck sometimes:

- Stuck in old stories and limiting beliefs that say, "I can't."
- Stuck in a boring job.
- Stuck for inspiration and creative solutions.
- Stuck in a destructive, repetitive pattern with family members, coworkers, or friends.

When we're stuck, we feel overwhelmed, afraid to take risks, even hopeless. The good news is: we are not.

In fact, we are extremely adept at getting unstuck, at seeing the same thing in new ways, discovering new insights and changing our attitudes, but we need some tools and strategies to create that movement.

Here are some of my favorite ways to get unstuck. Keep them all in your toolkit, or experiment to see which ones work most powerfully for you.

Eat **chocolate** | *Dance* | **Talk** to other experts | Stroll along the **beach** | Create a mind map | Plan an *artist's date* | Watch a **movie** | Soak in a bubble bath | ***Scribble and doodle*** | Read a book | **Work out** | WALK THE DOG | **Learn** something **new** | Ask myself: *Will this matter next week, next year?* | Listen to ***music*** | *Swing on a swing* | MEDITATE, PRAY | Call a friend. | *PLAY WITH A CHILD* | **Read my vision**

Make a list of twenty things you could do when you are stuck.

We Are the Torchbearers

RAE LUSKIN

Find your unique voice,

Paint a bold picture, and enthusiastically share it with others.

Move past fear, and step out in knowing,

Courageously claim what you value most.

Believe in a world where we are all interconnected,

Where women and children are well protected.

A world without suffering and pain,

Where love, respect, and peace reign.

Everyone helps protect the planet,

Disease and famine and war are no more

Change your thoughts and change the world,

An image of hope, and health and wealth for all.

Be a role model, mentor, or volunteer,

Pay it forward as a happiness harbinger,

A love luminary or a peace prophet,

A torchbearer of transformative vision

CHAPTER SIX

SET A GOOD EXAMPLE

"Setting an example is not the main means of influencing others; it's the only means."

–ALBERT EINSTEIN

It is vital to invest in future generations where every human being is fulfilling his or her greatest potential. We need to be role models and mentors. Our words, behaviors, and actions are the foundational building block for the adults of tomorrow, the people who are going to make the decisions, build the businesses, and run the world. We need to acknowledge their strengths and gifts, and help them to see that mistakes are steppingstones to success. Teach them to trust their feelings, and to share their voice. Help them to respect differences. We need to shift our conversations from impossible to possible. When we foster and encourage their dreams, we move toward a more sustainable and peaceful world.

It is imperative that we volunteer and share our valuable experience and expertise with others. We are meant to be of service to each other. We are happiest and healthiest when we help each other. Over the past two decades, a growing body of research indicates that volunteering provides individual health benefits, in addition to social ones. Those who volunteer had lower mortality rates, greater functional ability, and lower rates of depression later in life than those who do not volunteer.

The benefits of volunteering:

1. Model civic responsibility for your children.
2. Get to give back to your community.
3. Learn to solve real problems.
4. Connect to others in meaningful ways.
5. Save valuable resources.
6. Build self-esteem and confidence.
7. Reduces stress and makes you healthier and happier.
8. Get to learn something new.
9. Improve your leadership skills.

Volunteering helps us to tap into a sense of community. When you become involved in your community, you establish deep roots. Points of Light Institute revealed that when troubled youth were asked to do community service by helping younger children read and finish their homework, there was a startling transformation. The troubled children who volunteered skipped school less, avoided risky situations, and became more considerate of others. They concluded for the first time in their lives it gave them a sense of self-worth. By volunteering in the community, it instilled a pride and a sense of belonging.

Service is the energy that fuels our lives.

- According to Diane Osgood, when you vote with your conscience or your pocketbook, you have a greater impact than you think.

- Mary Robinson Reynolds encourages us to acknowledge and share how people make a difference in our lives.

- Mark Papadas helps our children believe in themselves.

- Kathy Eldon supports creative activists who tell stories that need to be told.

- Genevieve Fredrick improves the lives of thousands of homeless pets.

- Gilda Oliver brings people together through community art projects.

Each one of these unique, wonderful individuals has unleashed his or her passion and expertise, and made a positive change in the world. They are role models, mentors, and volunteers.

> "Never doubt that a small group of thoughtful committed citizens can change the world. Indeed, it is the only thing that ever has."

—MARGARET MEAD—

If you have a talent that you are passionate about, share it with other people.

GENEVIEVE FREDRICK IN 2007 FOUNDED PETS OF THE HOMELESS, AN ORGANIZATION THAT PROVIDES FOOD AND VETERINARY CARE FOR PETS OF HOMELESS PEOPLE THROUGHOUT THE UNITED STATES AND PARTS OF CANADA.

WHAT PROMPTED YOU TO CREATE PETS FOR THE HOMELESS?

When I visited New York City in 2006, I saw a homeless man on the sidewalk with a cane, begging. Lying next to him was a dog. I wondered why a guy who can barely feed himself would have a pet.

When I returned home to Carson City, Nevada, I couldn't forget the homeless man and his dog. I began researching the plight of homeless people and their pets. The research showed 5 to 10 percent of the nation's estimated 3.5 million homeless people have at least one pet. Because few shelters allow animals, most pet-owning homeless individuals sleep outdoors, in cars, and in tent camps to stay with their four-legged friends.

WHY DO YOU THINK SO MANY HOMELESS PEOPLE HAVE PETS?

Pets are loyal, nonjudgmental companions that provide comfort, even protection and warmth, and may be a homeless person's only companion. Many of the homeless had their pets before they were on the streets and wanted to keep them. During the Katrina disaster, you saw how many people would not leave their homes without their pets.

HOW DID YOU GET STARTED?

I asked my dog's veterinarians to collect pet-food donations. The local media picked up the story, and on the first day of collection, the donations filled a fifty-five-gallon trashcan. I created a website, and people started contacting me and sending money. I felt so uncomfortable with the money I called my attorney and had him file the paperwork for a nonprofit.

Since then, other businesses have joined the effort, and drives have spurred contributions. At last count, more than 322 tons of pet food have been donated. More than four hundred volunteers bring the food from 370 collection sites to be distributed at food banks, soup kitchens, and homeless shelters.

We work with veterinarians who volunteer their time to participate in wellness clinics. The organization provides funding to these vets to go out into homeless communities and administer vaccines, preventative treatments, and spay/neuter services.

Knowing that pets have a chance to get nutritious food and vet care makes all the years that I've devoted to the program worthwhile. Pets of the homeless don't choose their owners. But that doesn't matter, as long as they receive attention and love.

WHAT ARE YOUR GUIDING PRINCIPLES?

I have been an active Rotarian for years. They have served me well, and are the foundation for my relationships with family, friends, even strangers. Rotary fosters the ideal of service and uses this four-way test as an ethical guideline:

1. Is it the truth?
2. Is it fair to all concerned?
3. Will it build goodwill and better relationships?
4. Will it be beneficial to all concerned?

WHAT ONE THING WOULD YOU SAY TO SOMEBODY WHO SAID THEY WOULD LIKE TO MAKE A DIFFERENCE IN THE WORLD BUT DID NOT KNOW HOW?

First find your passion, whether it is music, animals, or people. What is your passion? What gives you joy? A retired teacher was staying with me, and she did not know what to do with her time. I asked her, "What did you enjoy the most in teaching?" She said she liked being around the children. I suggested with her background, she could volunteer in a local library and start a reading session for toddlers. She said that sounded perfect. When you retire, you still have a need to be needed and to make a contribution. Sometimes first it's the matter of talking to somebody, and then determining how much you will be able to give back. If you have a talent that you are passionate about, share it with other people.

PETSOFTHEHOMELESS.ORG

Journal:

- What are your guiding principles?

- What parts or activities do you enjoy in your job?

- If age, family obligations, and finances were not an issue, how would you spend your time and energy?

Call to Action:

Do one thing today toward helping your favorite cause.

- Like their Facebook page.

- Have a bake sale or fundraiser, and donate the proceeds.

- Create your own YouTube video about why you believe in the cause.

- Talk to your company about making a donation.

- Organize a brown bag lunch with coworkers and donate your lunch money.

- Tweet about them.

DIANE OSGOOD

Leadership is about connecting through love, and recognizing your own power to make something happen.

DIANE OSGOOD IS A RECOGNIZED SYSTEMS THINKER AND GLOBAL EXPERT IN SUSTAINABLE BUSINESS PRACTICES. SHE IS COFOUNDER OF THE SOULFUL ECONOMY MOVEMENT, WHICH IS A SYSTEM BASED ON CONSUMERISM THAT MAKES EVERYONE BETTER OFF. SHE BELIEVES THAT WE CAN HAVE AN ECONO-MY IN WHICH THERE ARE BETTER JOBS FOR MORE PEOPLE, MORE PEOPLE FIND CONNECTION AND A DEEPER SENSE OF HAPPINESS THROUGH THEIR MATERIAL PURCHASES, AND BUSINESSES GROW SUSTAINABLY. SHE IS THE BUSINESS IN-NOVATION DIRECTOR AT VIRGIN MANAGEMENT LIMITED AND HAS SERVED AS A SENIOR ADVISOR TO THE CLINTON GLOBAL INITIATIVE AND BUSINESS FOR SOCIAL RESPONSIBILITY. IN 2011 SHE WORKED CLOSELY WITH THE CLINTON GLOBAL INITIATIVE TO LAUNCH THE SUBJECT OF SUSTAINABLE CONSUMERISM ON THE GLOBAL AGENDA. SHE IS A BOARD MEMBER OF ALLIANCE TO STOP SLAVERY AND END TRAFFICKING (ASSET).

In 2011, she assisted Karama, a women's rights organization based in Cairo, in establishing the first-ever women's movement in Libya. It was an immediate and concrete response to the Arab Spring in order to empower women to play an equal part in the newly formed democracies in the Middle East.

WHAT IS YOUR DEFINITION OF LEADERSHIP?

I frequently think about the Martin Luther King quote: "Power without love is reckless and abusive, and love without power is sentimental and anemic." Leadership is about showing up 100 percent to what you do in the world, focusing on the next step, and owning your ability to cocreate change. Fundamentally, it's about connecting through love, and recognizing your own power to make something happen.

WHAT IS SOULFUL ECONOMY?

We believe we can change the economy with our shopping choices. We believe as individuals, we can make shopping choices that create more value, and as consumers, we vote for the world we want with each purchase. We can have an economy in which:

- We connect to the story of what we buy, making shopping more rewarding, and fostering a relationship between owners and producers.

- Better jobs are created for more people, as consumers come to increasingly value artisans, small-scale production, and brands that are committed to fair labor.

- Artisan and handmade is "the new luxury."

- Brands, businesses, and entrepreneurs generate sustainable profits.

- The environment is restored, not diminished.

This movement is about exciting and enabling us all to connect with our stuff, and value how it was made. We work with the supply-and-demand side to create real change. We believe we can build more value into the system for all.

HOW CAN WE MAKE A DIFFERENCE IN THE WORLD?

We each wear three hats:

1. As consumers, how we spend our money, what we purchase, what we know about our purchases, and how careful we are about purchasing.

2. How we vote, our citizenship, how we show up in local government, in our communities and in our states, and also in our federal level. Are we involved in local politics, do we get involved, how do we do so?

3. How we show up as employees or entrepreneurs.

Employees as citizens, and as consumers, are more powerful and influential than we think. For example, if you're passionate about ensuring that the people who produce our food are treated right, maybe you are passionate about having fair-trade coffee in your work cafeteria. You can have a huge impact and bring other people along when you explain the value. First you need to do the research, learn what other companies have done, and slowly build the case. Taking on such a project can be so fulfilling but also a frustrating, hard-learning journey. You can have a huge impact, much larger than we would ever think, because it's touched every employee's life. You set up a ripple effect. Now the company next door has to think three times before they say, "No, we can't do it."

SOULFUL-ECONOMY.COM

Journal:

- When have you been an advocate at work for something you believe in?
- How do you use your money to vote your conscience?
- What has inspired you to take a stand publicly?

Call to Action:

Learn the United Nations Millennium Goals Research ways you can get involved and make a difference, such as:

- Eradicate extreme poverty and hunger.
- Achieve universal primary education.
- Promote gender equality and empower women.
- Reduce child mortality.
- Improve maternal health.
- Combat HIV/AIDS, malaria, and other diseases.
- Ensure environmental stability.
- Develop a global partnership for development.

un.org/millenniumgoals

MARK PAPADAS

There are opportunities and resources out in front of you—be open to them.

MARK PAPADAS IS THE PRESIDENT AND CHIEF CREATIVE OFFICER OF I AM 4 KIDS. AFTER YEARS OF SUCCESSFULLY IMPROVING SALES TEAMS AND CREATING CUTTING-EDGE PROGRAMS FOR BUSINESSES, MARK DECIDED TO APPLY HIS KNOWLEDGE AND SKILLS TO EMPOWERING KIDS. HE CREATED I AM 4 KIDS, A REVOLUTIONARY PROGRAM THAT TEACHES SCHOOL-AGED KIDS HOW TO CREATE THEIR OWN EMPOWERING IDENTITY. IMAGINE TONY ROBBINS MEETS CHARLIE BROWN. ON THE GLOBAL SCALE, I AM 4 KIDS IS DOING FOR EMPOWERMENT AND DEVELOPMENT WHAT SESAME STREET DID FOR READING AND MATH. THE MISSION OF THE I AM 4 KIDS FOUNDATION IS TO IMPLEMENT THIS PROGRAM IN EVERY PUBLIC ELEMENTARY SCHOOL IN THE COUNTRY IN THE NEXT TEN YEARS AT NO COST TO THE SCHOOLS.

TELL ME ABOUT THE PROGRAM.

I AM 4 Kids came from a program I did with adults for about twelve years. It is a simple five-step process that I developed to build your own identity, and the first step is the same, whether you're a seven-year-old kid or a forty-seven-year-old CEO. The first step is to get a blank sheet of paper and write on it the words, "I am," and finish that statement. Immediately hands go up, whether it is a child or an adult, asking, "How do you want me to answer that? What are you looking for?" We say, "There's no right or wrong answer. Answer that however you think you should." Over 7 percent of the time, the adults would answer their name and/or occupation—neither of which has anything to do with who you are *as a person*.

In the pilot classrooms, we found that slightly over 50 percent of the kids answered with a one-word negative trait or characteristic, like, "I am stupid. I am fat. I am ugly. I am unlovable." We know adults build up behavioral patterns and belief systems, but kids are blank slates. Their only belief system is usually one given them, or they perceive, from the adults in their surroundings. They see how the adults act, and they may say, "Well, that's how I'm supposed to do it."

In our program, we are giving kids the opportunity to build their own belief system. We take them through a process to create an identity statement, and we anchor it with whole mind/body, mind work. The next step is to share and synergize it. We have the kids (or the adults) go home and tell mom, dad, aunts, uncles, brothers, sisters, and neighbors, anybody who will listen. We have created, for lack of a better term, a junior LinkedIn where they can post their identity statement anonymously. "I am an amazing person," and if a kid wants to connect with someone, the parents have to sign off and make it happen.

The final step is where the magic happens. The assignment: to pick a project that embodies the new identity you've created for yourself. The only rule is that it has to benefit somebody other than you. Some of these become exceptionally creative projects.

CAN YOU GIVE ME SOME EXAMPLES?

A little girl's father, unfortunately, was arrested on federal crime charges, and was serving time in prison. The family didn't have the money to go visit him on a regular basis, and it was not easy to phone. She wanted to design an Internet type of service that would allow video chat, specifically for kids to talk with their parents, so the parent could see them grow up even if he could not be there in person.

One little boy wanted to clean up his local park and paint the swing set. He needed fifteen gallons of paint. I called the local paint store and told them who we were, and we put this little boy on the phone who told the owner why he needed the paint. They donated the paint, and fifteen volunteers worked with him so he could see his project completed. This great model of success will take him far in life.

WHAT WOULD YOU SAY TO SOMEONE WHO SAYS HE WANTS TO MAKE A DIFFERENCE?

Find people who have done something similar to what you want. Study that person, but even more importantly, simply ask for help. This is who I am, what I want to accomplish, and will you help me do that? People are happy to help, and if they can't, they often make an introduction to someone who can. There are opportunities and resources out in front of you—be open to them.

IAM4KIDSFOUNDATION.ORG

Journal:

- How do you or your children answer this statement: I am . . . ?
- With whom can you share your identity statement?
- What kind of help do you need?

Call to Action:

Asking for help is tough. You worry if you ask for help you will look stupid, or you will owe the person you asked. It is not a sign of weakness. A smart person knows when she needs advice or assistance, and I love partnering with smart people.

People ask how I interviewed 120 people. My answer is I kept asking. I began interviewing people I knew in my inner circle in Chicago. I'd ask if they knew any other creative activists I should contact, and were they willing to make an introduction. People were genuinely thrilled to help. I was persistent, and did the research on LinkedIn and Facebook and found ways to connect with some of my heroes. If I heard an inspirational speaker, I tracked him down.

Create a safe space for people to tell their story. When you listen to someone's story with genuine curiosity, it creates openings for relationships. Over and over people said, "Wow, no one ever asked me that before. Those are great questions."

Make a list of five things you could ask for help with . . . and ask.

KATHY ELDON

My mission in life is to help people achieve their potential both for themselves, and for the world.

KATHY ELDON IS A JOURNALIST, FILM AND TELEVISION PRODUCER, TEACHER, AND AUTHOR WHO HAS WORKED IN ENGLAND, AFRICA, AND THE UNITED STATES. FOUNDER OF CREATIVE VISIONS PRODUCTIONS, WHICH PRODUCES ENTERTAINING SOCIALLY CONSCIOUS FILMS, INCLUDING *GLOBALTRIBE*, A PBS SERIES; *SOLDIERS OF PEACE: A CHILDREN'S CRUSADE* (CNN); *DYING TO TELL THE STORY*, AN EMMY-NOMINATED FILM ABOUT JOURNALISTS AT RISK (TBS); *EXTRAORDINARY MOMS*, FEATURING JULIA ROBERTS, HILLARY CLINTON, AND CHRISTIANE AMANPOUR (OWN); AND A FAMILY FEATURE, *LOST IN AFRICA*, DISTRIBUTED BY COLUMBIA. SHE'S CURRENTLY PRODUCING *BEST CARE POSSIBLE*, ABOUT END-OF-LIFE CARE IN AMERICA FOR PBS, AND *JOURNEY*, ABOUT HER SON, DAN ELDON, A REUTERS PHOTOGRAPHER KILLED IN SOMALIA IN 1993. IN 2013 KATHY PUBLISHED HER MEMOIR, *IN THE HEART OF LIFE*, IN WHICH SHE SHARES THE POWER OF THE HUMAN SPIRIT.

WHAT WAS BEHIND CREATIVE VISIONS?

I learned about creative activism in Africa. In the mid-eighties, so many writers, artists, and musicians in the nation were issue-oriented. Focused on the power of media to inform, inspire, and empower change, I started a production company called Creative Visions. We produced a film about elephant poaching.

When Dan was killed in Somalia at age twenty-two while taking photos for Reuters, my daughter, Amy, and I started a foundation to celebrate the creative activist experience I had seen in others, and certainly in Dan. Since its inception in 1997, we have assisted over two hundred artists, filmmakers, playwrights, and leaders of social movement on five continents to impact over 100 million people. If you want to move society and culture in positive ways, we must understand how to tell stories—about problems that need to be solved—and get them to the widest audience. Also, we need to tell them what to do to help. Ideas are wonderful, but we need action to truly transform things.

Initially we supported a number of independent filmmakers with small grants. In 2004 we recognized that we could support them better by creating a kind of community around them by providing physical sponsorship, as well as supporting their visions and their dreams by connecting them with other likeminded people, mentors, or lawyers, and whatever it was they needed.

My self-appointed job in life is to help people achieve their potential, both for themselves and for the world. During the day I see four or five young people, who I call "sparks of light," and I love to help them see that they can have a role in changing the world around them.

HOW DO YOU DEFINE CREATIVE ACTIVIST?

The logo for Creative Visions is the first hexagram of the I Ching, an ancient Chinese divination technique. It is made up of six unbroken lines, which stand for primal creative power and action to create social change. To be an activist, at times you have to stand still and bide your time, but primarily you are figuring out how to get from point A to point B in the most effective and efficient way and bringing along as many people as you can. You have to be a lateral thinker, a very creative thinker. To be an activist means you are stepping outside of whatever boxes you were born into and are looking sideways and around corners, trying to figure out how you can create a solution that also engages others in the communication and implementation of that solution.

WHAT IS YOUR VISION FOR THE FUTURE?

I want to get our Rock Your World curriculum to every school in America, and work with UNESCO to get it around the world. Rock Your World is an innovative, multi-dimensional, project-based curriculum for middle and high school students, and it engages them in real-world issues. It was born out of our PBS series *GlobalTribe* in which we interviewed visionaries and social entrepreneurs from around the world. It was piloted for four years in New York and Australia, with over six thousand participants.

First we teach our students about human rights, and then we give them ample time to explore a variety of issues until they identify one that "sparks" or inspires them to action. We ask students to consider how human rights relate to themselves, their community, country, and the world. We encourage them to ask brave questions about the challenges they see in their neighborhoods and the world around them, and we help position them to work positively to overcome those challenges. It is a process of researching an issue of interest and developing an "action campaign" to address it. Designed with multiple entry points, and fully aligned with Common Core and state standards, the program features a comprehensive curriculum guide and the resources to help students create a persuasive public service announcement, using digital media to promote their designated cause.

CREATIVEVISIONS.ORG

Journal:

- What inspires you to action?
- What films have inspired you to research a subject more thoroughly?
- What makes a public service announcement compelling and effective?

Call to Action:

One of my heroes is Eleanor Roosevelt. She was appointed a delegate to the United Nations after the death of her husband, President Franklin D. Roosevelt. She brought to the commission her commitment to human dignity and compassion, her experience in lobbying and politics, and her concern for refugees after World War II. She worked on a Universal Declaration of Human Rights, writing part of the text, helping to frame the language and keep it focused on human dignity. On December 10, 1948, the General Assembly of the United Nations adopted a resolution endorsing the Universal Declaration of Human Rights.

In her speech before that General Assembly, Eleanor Roosevelt said:

We stand today at the threshold of a great event both in the life of the United Nations and in the life of mankind. This declaration may well become the international Magna Carta for all men everywhere. We hope its proclamation by the General Assembly will be an event comparable to the proclamation in 1789 (the French Declaration of the Rights of Citizens), the adoption of the Bill of Rights by the people of the U.S., and the adoption of comparable declarations at different times in other countries.

Read the declaration: un.org/en/documents/udhr/index.shtml/

MARY ROBINSON REYNOLDS

It is critical to the world, our communities, and families that we acknowledge three people every day.

MARY ROBINSON REYNOLDS SPENT HER EARLY PROFESSIONAL YEARS AS A K-8 TEACHER BEFORE BECOMING A K-12 COUNSELOR. SHE HAD TREMENDOUS AND MEASURABLE ACADEMIC SUCCESS WITH CHILDREN WHO HAD BEEN WRITTEN OFF BY THE SYSTEM. SHE DEVELOPED "ATTITUDINAL" ENERGY TECHNIQUES TO EMPOWER STUDENTS AND THEIR PARENTS TO EFFECTIVELY BRIDGE COMMUNI-CATIONS AND LEADERSHIP WITHIN THE EDUCATIONAL SYSTEM.

IN 2006 SHE DISCOVERED ONLINE MOVIES AS A MEDIUM FOR INSPIRATIONAL STORYTELLING THAT TOUCHES THE HEART AND INSPIRES THE SPIRIT. IN 2007, MARY WAS INTRODUCED TO HELICE "SPARKY" BRIDGES BY ONE OF HER OWN SUBSCRIBERS, AND THE TWO WOMEN JOINED THEIR INTENTIONS TO MAKE THE WORLD A BETTER PLACE THROUGH HEART PRODUCTIONS & PUBLISHING. THEY CREATED *THE ACKNOWLEDGMENT MOVIE.*

"I've learned that people will forget what you said, people will forget what you did, but people will never forget how you made them feel."

—MAYA ANGELOU—

WHAT IS *THE ACKNOWLEDGEMENT MOVIE* ABOUT?

Briefly, a high school teacher in New York decides to honor her seniors by telling them how they made a difference. She also gave them a blue ribbon that said, "Who I am makes a difference." She passed out three blue ribbons, and asked everyone to "pass it forward" as an experiment. One young man had a mentor, and told him how much his help meant in career planning. He pinned on the ribbon, and asked him to pass it on. The man went to his boss, who was kind of gruff most of the time, and told him he was a creative genius. He asked him to wear a ribbon, and take the last one to honor someone. The boss went home that night and sat down with his son and explained what happened. "I don't tell you enough how proud I am of you, and that you and your mom are the most important people in my life." The young man began to cry. "I didn't think you loved me, and I was going to kill myself tonight."

The boss was a changed man. He made sure he told his employees how they made a difference. The junior executive continued to mentor. Everyone learned that who you are does make a difference.

WHY DO YOU THINK YOU WERE SO SUCCESSFUL WITH CHILDREN?

My parents were very old school, very rigid, regimented, and harsh. They were verbally and physically abusive, which was acceptable in those days. I made a very conscious choice I would never treat my children the way I was treated. I was so successful with at-risk children because I listened to them. I tapped into their greatness, and refused to label them negatively, like I had been labeled. In addition, I set up my classrooms as kinesthetic learning experiences.

WHY IS ACKNOWLEDGMENT SO IMPORTANT?

When I was in grad school, I was going through a very rough time, looking for love in all the wrong places, and struggling with school. My counselor gave me this assignment: for thirty days you need to touch someone; it can be a pat on the back, a verbal acknowledgment, or a virtual hug. It was challenging and painful in the beginning—but it changed my life. When we do this, it transforms our own life, and our circle of influence. When we grow and celebrate each other's dreams, goals, and accomplishments, people will step into their greatness and their authentic self.

Gandhi's famous quote, *"Be the change you want to see in the world,"* is so true. One decision to change our personal world can end up inspiring others to do the same. It is critical to the world, our communities, and families that we acknowledge three people every day.

MAKEADIFFERENCE.COM

Journal:

- What teacher had a major influence on your life, and why?

- Who would you like to pass your blue ribbons to, and why?

- How can you help someone step into his or her greatness?

Call to Action:

Starting today, make a point to acknowledge and thank one family member and one friend every day for a week. Tell them how important they are to you, and how they have made a difference in your life. You can drop by and thank them in person, or send a letter or a card. While we all have busy lives, the connections we have to one another are what matter most. Make a call, send a text, or email.

GILDA OLIVER

Art builds a bridge of diplomacy.

GILDA OLIVER IS A RENOWNED CERAMIST, SCULPTOR, PAINTER, AND TEACH-
ER WHO HAS BEEN IN THE TRENCHES OF CREATIVITY FOR YEARS. HER WORK
IS A SOCIAL FORCE THAT ATTRACTS PUBLIC ATTENTION, WITH PARTICIPANTS
COMING FROM MOSCOW TO MANHATTAN. SHE'S THE DIRECTOR AND FACILI-
TATOR OF MAJOR LARGE-SCALE MOSAIC ART PROJECTS. THE PROJECTS INTE-
GRATE CHILDREN AND ADULTS IN ARTISTIC EXPRESSION, AND THIS COMMU-
NITY MOVES BEYOND GEOPOLITICAL BOUNDARIES, REVEALING ELEMENTS OF
SPIRITUAL LIFE, MYSTICISM, AND NATURE.

HOW DO YOU GET SPONSORS?

Today they come to me. I have been blessed to have Courage Lion Unlimited and
Champions for the Challenged as sponsors who have supported my last four mural
projects. They have provided financial support, and more. On any given day, one of
their board members can be found working on the sprawling mosaics in a three-
piece suit, then running out to a budget meeting, and back to the mosaic. I like to
think they have also been changed by their participation.

For six weeks during the summer of 2011, volunteers of all ages helped to create beautiful ceramic tiles to contribute to Love Over the Rainforest. Children and their families made hundreds of colorful animals and plants that were fired, glazed, and placed within the mosaic. To complete the jungle scene, small square tiles and glass beads were cemented down before colored grout filled in the gaps. What wonderful bonds and friendships the people working together on the project made.

WHY IS ART SO IMPORTANT?

Art touches people's spirits. At one point everything we wore, gave as gifts, or used was made by hand or found in nature. Art, dance, and storytelling were personal expressions and a connection with nature and other people. When people come together and make tiles, the combined force radiates positive energy and color into the world. That is why community murals have such a powerful effect on those who participate, and those who come to see them. Participants realize they are beautiful inside, and are recognized for the gifts and contribution to community. One boy was a quadriplegic, and he told the staff where to put his dove—just because he couldn't do it physically didn't matter. He contributed.

WHAT ARE YOU WORKING ON NOW?

Currently I am working on a community-assisted arts-based project that will first be displayed at the Baltimore Port Children's Museum. It is a mosaic and clay tile mural, nine by twenty feet, created at a Baltimore school for challenged students. This piece is significantly different from previous pieces I have designed and executed with community volunteers. First, the previous mosaics were permanently installed on museum walls as part of local community outreach. This project will be placed on a steel frame by Pierce Steel, and will travel around the world to different museums. With each community project, I have tried to increase the scope and the difficulty of the project. The goal is for the community to evolve to meet the challenge of discovering art built in daily life, and the value of a vision.

WHAT IS YOUR GOAL FOR THE FUTURE?

I would like to go into new communities to bring recognition to great artists, young and old. Projects like mine attract a diverse and talented workforce that contributes to public culture. People desire to live where great art is created and exhibited. Finding funding, volunteers, and display space is a challenge. Often I personally have to help fill in the financial gaps.

My next project is a new medium for me. In Baltimore we are creating a student/family/community fabric art mural. Fundraising helped me purchase a ten-by-ten-foot black satin quilt as the frame of the mosaic. The students and parents will sew their border design to the edge of the project, using a loaned sewing machine. A fragile log cabin front piece will be sewn by hand as is in the center. It will be donated to the Baltimore Regional Lewis Museum of African American History and Culture. My goal is to see the individual creativity blossom in my project participants. The mural art is a spiritual vessel, and a high-quality public artwork, which now publically celebrates their vision and accomplishment.

GILDAOLIVER.COM

Journal:

- How does art touch your spirit?
- If there were no limitations, what is the grandest vision you can imagine for your cause or project?
- Who could you invite to be a community partner?

Call to Action:

Participate in a community art project. It could be an art exhibit or mural painting, cards for veterans for the Fourth of July, or making quilts for cancer patients at your local hospital. Contact your local arts council for a list of ongoing projects.

If you want to volunteer abroad, research At Projects Abroad, which gives you the opportunity to forge real connections with real people in the country in which you volunteer, using and developing your skills in music, dance, building, or working alongside people in unique environments such as Vietnamese stilt villages or with Moroccan nomads on the edge of the Sahara.

projects-abroad.com.au/projects/culture-and-community

The Power of One

RAE LUSKIN

One smile can brighten someone's day

One word can start a dialogue

One "I forgive you" can heal a heart

One "I'm sorry" can reconcile a relationship

One loving conversation can transform a life

One act of kindness can inspire the next generation

One individual standing up for another can create community

One minute of stillness can connect you to Divine Love

One act of peace can send out ripples of hope

One new idea can spark a hundred

One vote of conscience can inform policy

One act of collaboration can cause sweeping change

One person can make a difference

CONCLUSION
Where do we go from here?

> *"We make a living by what we get.*
> *We make a life by what we give."*
>
> -WINSTON CHURCHILL-

You have been introduced to creative activists, thirty-six ordinary people doing extraordinary things. If you have done the inner work and taken the action steps along the way, you should feel more confident and empowered and wake up every day feeling more energized, inspired, and motivated because you know you are making the world a better place. Being grounded in your passion and core values makes your life have more meaning and direction. You are adept at generating new ideas and solutions. You know how to engage people in your big, bold vision. You know you have something that is uniquely yours to give.

WHAT IS STOPPING YOU?

Recently I attended Mary Morrissey's Dream Builder Live conference. One of the most compelling experiences of the weekend happened on the last day. We were examining our fears—the things that kept us from going after our dreams. We broke into groups of three. For one minute, one person on each side of you would say in your ear all the things you say to yourself over and over, like: *You are stupid, lazy, crazy, and not enough, who do you think you are, you will never make money, and you are a failure.* I hated saying all those things to another human being, but they rolled off my tongue with ease because it is what I have said to myself.

The second part of the activity was for people to say only wonderful things about you: *You are brave, courageous, warm and tender, wise, smart and empathetic, and successful.* I burst into tears hearing those words, and I felt this opening in my heart and a shift in my body and how I saw myself in relationship to the other people in the room.

When we believe we are "good enough," our inclination is to reach out to those in need. When we recognize our incredible beauty, and our divine spirit, we can be truly generous. When we come from a place of appreciation, joy, and inner peace, it is like a love letter to the world.

What is the love letter you are sending? What is the message of your heart? Whom are you sending it to? Remember, one person can make a difference. You are a force of nature, and you're more powerful than you think. Start where you are, with what you have, maybe a smile and a kind word. Helping people feel valued is one of the most precious gifts you can give.

From an early age, I was very lucky my family instilled within me an ethic of service to the community. Not everyone feels that way, or has been exposed to this idea. Your life may have been filled with challenges and disappointments, and you feel the world owes you. Yet you might recognize if someone reached out and lent a helping hand, your life would have been different. Now is the time to give back. Know that you matter, and what you do matters. You make a difference.

Finally, tell your story. Sharing your voice is important to your personal growth, and to your ability to make a difference. When you share your brilliance, power, and purpose, your soul lights up. People are faced with numerous challenges and transitions today. People feel stuck in unfulfilling marriages, or are taking care of aging parents, have been laid off, or are facing retirement, and still want to be valuable and contributing citizens. They are hungering to create more, give more, and connect on a deeper level. They are starving for guidance and inspiration. If you have solved a problem, organized a group, been a leader, created a unique product to advance social change or an inspired piece of art for your neighborhood, school, workplace, or congregation, you have probably learned some invaluable lessons.

Last year I attended the Chicago Ideas Week Instigator Lecture. I was amazed and touched by the depth and breadth of what creative activists are doing in Chicago and around the world: a model committed to better maternal healthcare, a basketball star talking about the power of knowing someone's name, circus performers raising money for renovating park districts, confiscated guns turned into jewelry to help fund anti-gun programs.

You have your own ideas and visions, solutions and expertise, about how to live better lives and create positive change. It is time to share them. While it may seem scary to share your individual voice with the world, people are more supportive than you think. The first time I told my story, my knees were knocking, I stumbled a few times on the words, and my voice shook, yet no one judged me. I will never forget the woman who came up to me afterwards and said, "You saved my life." People will admire and appreciate you for sharing your experience and wisdom.

If you want to continue the legacy of the creative activist, please share your story on our Creative Activists Facebook page. We would love to hear from you. This will be a storehouse of ideas, inspiration, practical tools, and guidance as to how you can solve problems and make a difference in the world.

> ## "I alone cannot change the world, but I can cast a stone across the water to create many ripples."
>
> —MOTHER TERESA—

ABOUT THE AUTHOR

Rae is a true leader in using creative expression to nurture self-worth, resilience, healing, and social change. For over fifteen years, Rae has helped individuals and teams uncover their unique talents and passions in order to become confident leaders. She has a bachelor of fine arts degree from Roosevelt University and a master's degree from Loyola University in urban planning. She has been a community activist since she was twenty-three, and finds ways to balance her artistic side and her desire to improve the lives of women and families. She is committed to being the change she wants to see in the world. She is the author of *Art from My Heart*, a creative self-discovery journal published in 2010. She is a contributing author to *Shine the Light: Sexual Abuse and Healing in the Jewish Community* by Rachel Lev and *Learning from Failure: 11 Sure Fire Ways to Turn Your Worst Failures into Your Biggest Success*. As a speaker, educator, and mentor, Rae loves to lead workshops. Her most popular programs are Chocolate, Creativity and Change; Discover the Creative Edge; and Make the World Better: One Person, One Action at a Time.

Rae loves to hear from readers! If you would like to be in touch with her, please email Rae at rae@thewinningadventure.com or call 847-948-0315.

THEWINNINGADVENTURE.COM

Twitter: **@RaeLuskin** | Facebook Group: **/CreativeActivists**